Law Enforcement

LAW ENFORCEMENT

A Selective Bibliography

————

EMANUEL T. PROSTANO

and

MARTIN L. PICCIRILLO

1974

————

LIBRARIES UNLIMITED, INC.

Littleton, Colo.

Library of Congress Card Number 73-86399
International Standard Book Number 0-87287-077-4

LIBRARIES UNLIMITED, INC.
P.O. Box 263
Littleton, Colorado 80120

TABLE OF CONTENTS

INTRODUCTION

The law enforcement field, which is concerned with total requirements for effective police service in our society, is considered one element in the American criminal justice system. The pattern of organization of the law enforcement field is similar to that of the overall political system in America. There are independent, yet overlapping, areas of interest, responsibility, and authority. Law enforcement consists of governmental units at federal, state, county, and municipal levels as well as regional jurisdictional units. There are governmental auxiliary, honorary, reserve, and voluntary units. Additionally, one may consider the broad, complex private enterprise as an element of the law enforcement field.

Those functioning in the law enforcement field are primarily interested in the following areas: 1) *Police Science*, which includes planning, organization, management and supervision, patrol and traffic operations, criminal investigation and criminalistics; 2) *Law*, including constitutional law, criminal law, and related areas such as vehicle, domestic, and municipal law; 3) *Behavioral and Social Sciences*, including sociology, psychology, criminology and juvenile delinquency; 4) *Training*, including physical training and self-defense, weapons training, crowd control, disaster procedures, first aid, and vehicular training. Beyond the law enforcement field *per se*, interest encompasses the total criminal justice field and even, in a multi-disciplinary fashion, the entire range of man's knowledge.

This volume contains selected publications which fall into the purview of the law enforcement field. Entries span the period 1967 through 1972. The year 1967 was used as a starting point because it was then that the President's Commission on Law Enforcement and Administration of Justice[1] set new goals and directions for the field.

Books, pamphlets, and various audiovisual media are included in the main section of the work, and a list of serials is also provided.

ORGANIZATION

The subject categories employed in this work are those used in the *Thesaurus*[2] of the National Criminal Justice Reference Service (NCJRS). The *Thesaurus* contains various listings of terms by which documents are indexed and retrieved.

In the body of the work, entries are listed alphabetically under the various subject indicators. As a key to multi-disciplinary works, "see also" cross references are cited under each subject indicator to suggest other appropriate subjects to be searched by the user. The "subject/content indicators-hierarchic" section of the NCJRS *Thesaurus* is reproduced as an appendix to the work. The 250 starred titles are those that are highly recommended.

The volume should be of interest and value to those who function at an operational level in law enforcement and other elements of the criminal justice system. It will also serve as a useful guide for institutions offering law enforcement, criminal justice, law, and behavioral and social science programs. Public and academic libraries will find the work useful in extending their resource collections to accommodate the needs of yet another segment of society.

We wish to extend our thanks and appreciation to Elaine S. Mazeika for typing the manuscript.

E.T.P.

M.L.P.

FOOTNOTES

[1] President's Commission on Law Enforcement and Administration of Justice, *The Challenge of Crime in a Free Society* (Washington, U.S. Government Printing Office, 1967).

[2] National Criminal Justice Reference Service, *Thesaurus* (Washington, U.S. Law Enforcement Assistance Administration, U.S. Department of Justice, 1972).

To: Lori, Steve, Joyce

E.T.P.

To: Marta, Louis, Conrad, Paula, and our parents

M.L.P.

ALCOHOLISM

See also **Domestic Relations**   **Police Traffic Function**
Drug Information/Treatment   **Support Services**
Judicial Process

1. Al-Anon Family Group. AL-ANON FACES ALCOHOLISM. New York, N.Y.: Al-Anon Family Group Headquarters, 1968.

2. American Medical Association. ALCOHOL AND THE IMPAIRED DRIVER. Chicago, Ill.: American Medical Association, 1970.

3. Cahalan, Don. AMERICAN DRINKING PRACTICES: A NATIONAL STUDY OF DRINKING BEHAVIOR AND ATTITUDES. New Brunswick, N.J.: Rutgers Center for Alcohol Studies, 1969.

4. Cahn, Sidney. TREATMENT OF ALCOHOLICS: AN EVALUATIVE STUDY. New York, N.Y.: Oxford University Press, 1970.

★ 5. Catanzaro, Ronald (ed.). ALCOHOLISM: THE TOTAL TREATMENT APPROACH. Springfield, Ill.: Charles C. Thomas, 1972.

6. Chafetz, Morris, and others (eds.). FRONTIERS OF ALCOHOLISM. New York, N.Y.: Science House, 1970.

7. Cook, T., and others. THE DRUNKENNESS OFFENSE. Elmsford, N.Y.: Pergamon Press, 1969.

★ 8. Corrigan, Eileen. ALCOHOLICS SEEKING TREATMENT. New Brunswick, N.J.: Rutgers Center for Alcohol Studies, 1972.

9. THE EFFECTS OF ALCOHOL. (Sound filmstrip, color.) Gaithersburg, Md.: International Association of Chiefs of Police.

10. Forney, Robert B., and Francis W. Hughes. COMBINED EFFECTS OF ALCOHOL AND OTHER DRUGS. Springfield, Ill.: Charles C. Thomas, 1968.

11. Grad, Frank P. ALCOHOLISM AND THE LAW. Dobbs Ferry, N.Y.: Oceana Publications, 1970.

12. Hirsh, Joseph. OPPORTUNITIES AND LIMITATIONS IN THE TREATMENT OF ALCOHOLICS. Springfield, Ill.: Charles C. Thomas, 1967.

13. Keller, John. DRINKING PROBLEM. Philadelphia, Pa.: Fortress Press, 1971.

14. Kent, Patricia. AN AMERICAN WOMAN AND ALCOHOL. New York, N.Y.: Holt Rinehart and Winston, 1967.

15. Ludwig, Arnold, and others. LSD AND ALCOHOLISM: A CLINICAL STUDY OF TREATMENT EFFICACY. Springfield, Ill.: Charles C. Thomas, 1970.

16. MANUAL ON ALCOHOLISM. Chicago, Ill.: American Medical Association, 1968.

17. Nimmer, R. T. TWO MILLION UNNECESSARY ARRESTS— REMOVING A SOCIAL SERVICE CONCERN FROM THE CRIMINAL JUSTICE SYSTEM. Chicago, Ill.: American Bar Foundation, 1971.

18. Pittman, David J. ALCOHOLISM. Scranton, Pa.: Harper and Row, 1967.

19. Plaut, Thomas F. (ed.). ALCOHOL PROBLEMS: A REPORT TO THE NATION BY THE COOPERATIVE COMMISSION ON THE STUDY OF ALCOHOLISM. New York, N.Y.: Oxford University Press, 1967.

* 20. President's Commission on Law Enforcement and Administration of Justice. DRUNKENNESS: TASK FORCE REPORT. Washington, D.C.: U.S. Government Printing Office, 1967.

21. Ritson, Bruce, and Christine Hassal. MANAGEMENT OF ALCOHOLISM. Baltimore, Md.: Williams and Wilkins, 1970.

22. Spradley, James P. YOU OWE YOURSELF A DRUNK: AN ETHNOGRAPHY OF URBAN NOMADS. Waltham, Mass.: Little Brown and Co., 1970.

23. Stewart, Ernest, and James Malfetti. REHABILITATION OF THE DRUNKEN DRIVER: A CORRECTIVE COURSE IN PHOENIX, ARIZONA FOR PERSONS CONVICTED OF DRIVING UNDER THE INFLUENCE OF ALCOHOL. New York, N.Y.: Teachers College Press, 1970.

24. Strachan, J. C. ALCOHOLISM: TREATABLE ILLNESS. New York, N.Y.: William S. Heinman, 1968.

25. Trice, Harrison. ALCOHOLISM IN AMERICA. New York, N.Y.: McGraw-Hill, 1967.

26. U.S. Department Health, Education, & Welfare.
ALCOHOL EDUCATION, CONFERENCE PROCEEDINGS.
Washington, D.C.: U.S. Government Printing Office, 1967.

★ 27. U.S. Law Enforcement Assistance Administration. ALCOHOL AND
THE CRIMINAL JUSTICE SYSTEM: CHALLENGE AND
RESPONSE. Washington, D.C.: U.S. Law Enforcement Assistance
Administration, 1972.

28. Whitney, Elizabeth (ed.). WORLD DIALOGUE ON ALCOHOL
AND DRUG DEPENDENCE. Boston, Mass.: Beacon Press, 1970.

29. Wilkinson, Rupert. PREVENTION OF DRINKING PROBLEMS:
ALCOHOL CONTROL AND CULTURAL INFLUENCES. New
York, N.Y.: Oxford University Press, 1970.

BEHAVIORAL AND SOCIAL SCIENCES

See also Civil Rights
Criminology
Domestic Relations
Drug Information/Treatment
Judicial Process

Juvenile Delinquency
Laws and Statutes
Riot Control and Urban
 Disorders
Student Disorders
Support Services

★ 30. Abbott, David W., and others. POLICE, POLITICS AND RACE:
THE NEW YORK CITY REFERENDUM ON CIVILIAN REVIEW.
Cambridge, Mass.: Harvard University Press, 1969.

31. Abrahamsen, David. OUR VIOLENT SOCIETY. New York, N.Y.:
Funk and Wagnalls Co., 1970.

32. Adrian, Charles. STATE AND LOCAL GOVERNMENTS. New York,
N.Y.: McGraw-Hill, 1971.

33. Advisory Committee on Intergovernmental Relations. URBAN
AMERICA AND THE FEDERAL SYSTEM. Washington, D.C.:
U.S. Government Printing Office, 1969.

34. Aiken, Michael, and others. ECONOMIC FAILURE, ALIENATION,
AND EXTREMISM. Ann Arbor, Mich.: University of Michigan
Press, 1968.

35. Alexander, Theron. CHILDREN AND ADOLESCENTS: A BIOLOG-
ICAL APPROACH TO PSYCHOLOGICAL DEVELOPMENT.
Chicago, Ill.: Aldine/Atherton, 1969.

14   BEHAVIORAL AND SOCIAL SCIENCES

36. Alinsky, Saul. RULES FOR RADICALS. Westminster, Md.: Random House, 1971.

37. Allen, Clifford. A TEXTBOOK OF PSYCHOSEXUAL DISORDERS. New York, N.Y.: Oxford University Press, 1969.

38. Allen, Gary. COMMUNIST REVOLUTION IN THE STREETS. Belmont, Mass.: Western Islands, 1967.

39. Allsop, Kenneth. HARD TRAVELLIN': THE HOBO AND HIS HISTORY. New York, N.Y.: New American Library, 1970.

40. Anderson, S. OMBUDSMEN FOR AMERICAN GOVERNMENT. Englewood Cliffs, N.J.: Prentice Hall, 1968.

41. Anthony, Earl. PICKING UP THE GUN: A REPORT ON THE BLACK PANTHERS. New York, N.Y.: Dial Press, 1970.

42. Argyris, Chris. INTERVENTION THEORY AND METHOD: A BEHAVIORAL SCIENCE VIEW. Reading, Mass.: Addison-Wesley, 1970.

43. Arnold, David. THE SOCIOLOGY OF SUBCULTURES. Berkeley, Calif.: Glendessary Press, 1970.

44. Aronfreed, Justin. CONDUCT AND CONSCIENCE: SOCIALIZATION OF INTERNALIZED CONTROL OVER BEHAVIOR. New York, N.Y.: Academic Press, 1968.

45. Ashley-Montagu, M. F. (ed.). MAN AND AGGRESSION. New York, N.Y.: Oxford University Press, 1968.

46. Aukofer, Frank. CITY WITH A CHANCE. St. Paul, Minn.: Bruce Publishing Co., 1968.

47. Banfield, Edward C. THE UNHEAVENLY CITY: THE NATURE AND FUTURE OF OUR URBAN CRISIS. Waltham, Mass.: Little Brown & Co., 1970.

48. Banovetz, James. MANAGING THE MODERN CITY. Washington, D.C.: International City Managers Association, 1971.

★ 49. Banton, Michael. RACE RELATIONS. New York, N.Y.: Basic Books, 1968.

50. Barbara, Dominick A. YOUR SPEECH REVEALS YOUR PERSONALITY. Springfield, Ill.: Charles C. Thomas, 1970.

51. Barbour, Floyd (ed.). THE BLACK SEVENTIES. Boston, Mass.: Porter Sargent Publishers, 1970.

52. Barron, Milton L. MINORITIES IN A CHANGING WORLD. New York, N.Y.: Alfred A. Knopf, 1967.

53. Barton, Allen H. COMMUNITIES IN DISASTER: A SOCIOLOGI- CAL ANALYSIS OF COLLECTIVE STRESS SITUATIONS. Garden City, N.Y.: Doubleday & Co., 1969.

54. Baruch, Ruth-Marion, and Pirkle Jones. THE VANGUARD: A PHOTOGRAPHIC ESSAY ON THE BLACK PANTHERS. Boston, Mass.: Beacon Press, 1970.

55. Baughman, Earl E. BLACK AMERICANS, A PSYCHOLOGICAL ANALYSIS. New York, N.Y.: Academic Press, 1971.

★ 56. Bayley, David H., and H. Mendelsohn. MINORITIES AND THE POLICE. Riverside, N.J.: Free Press, 1971.

57. Bayton, James A. TENSION IN THE CITIES: THREE PROGRAMS FOR SURVIVAL. Philadelphia, Pa.: Chilton Books, 1969.

58. Bell, Carolyn. THE ECONOMICS OF THE GHETTO. Indianapolis, Ind.: Pegasus, 1970.

59. Bell, Inge Powell. CORE AND THE STRATEGY OF NON- VIOLENCE. Westminster, Md.: Random House, 1968.

60. Bellens, John, and Henry Schmandt. THE METROPOLIS: ITS PEOPLE, POLITICS AND ECONOMIC LIFE. New York, N.Y.: Harper and Row, 1970.

61. Bellush, Jewell, and Stephen David. RACE AND POLITICS IN NEW YORK CITY. New York, N.Y.: Praeger Publishers, 1970.

62. Berger, Peter L., and Richard J. Neuhaus. MOVEMENT AND REVOLUTION: A CONVERSATION ON AMERICAN RADICAL- ISM. Garden City, N.Y.: Doubleday and Co., 1970.

63. Berger, Peter M. CHRONOLOGICAL HISTORY OF THE NEGRO IN AMERICA. New York, N.Y.: New American Library, 1970.

64. Bergman, Rita E. SOCIOPATH: SELECTIONS IN ANTI-SOCIAL BEHAVIOR. Jericho, N.Y.: Exposition Press, 1968.

65. Berkovitz, Irving (ed.). ADOLESCENTS GROW IN GROUPS: CLINICAL EXPERIENCES IN ADOLESCENT GROUP PSYCHO- THERAPY. New York, N.Y.: Brunner/Mazel, 1972.

66. Berkowitz, Leonard. ROOTS OF AGGRESSION, A RE-EXAMINATION OF THE FRUSTRATION-AGGRESSION HYPOTH-ESIS. Chicago, Ill.: Aldine/Atherton, 1969.

★ 67. Bernstein, Saul. ALTERNATIVES TO VIOLENCE. New York, N.Y.: Associated Press, 1970.

68. Bienen, Henry. VIOLENCE AND SOCIAL CHANGE. Chicago, Ill.: University of Chicago Press, 1969.

69. Bierstedt, Robert. SOCIAL ORDER: AN INTRODUCTION TO SOCIOLOGY. New York, N.Y.: McGraw-Hill, 1970.

70. BIG BROTHER AND THE NOW GENERATION (Cassette tape, 29 min.) North Hollywood, Calif.: Center for Cassette Studies.

71. Billingsley, Andrew. BLACK FAMILIES IN WHITE AMERICA. Englewood Cliffs, N.J.: Prentice Hall, 1968.

★ 72. Blalock, Hubert M., Jr. TOWARD A THEORY OF MINORITY GROUP RELATIONS. New York, N.Y.: G. P. Putnam's Sons, 1970.

★ 73. Bloch, Herbert A., and Melvin Prince. SOCIAL CRISIS AND DEVIANCE: THEORETICAL FOUNDATIONS. Westminster, Md.: Random House, 1967.

74. Boorstin, Daniel J. THE DECLINE OF RADICALISM: REFLEC-TIONS ON AMERICA TODAY. Westminster, Md.: Random House, 1969.

75. Booth, Alan, and John Edwards. SOCIAL PARTICIPATION IN URBAN SOCIETY. Cambridge, Mass.: Schenkman Publishing Co., 1972.

76. Borgatta, Edgar. SOCIOLOGICAL METHODOLOGY. San Francisco, Calif.: Jossey-Bass, 1970.

★ 77. Boskin, Joseph. URBAN RACIAL VIOLENCE IN THE TWENTIETH CENTURY. Riverside, N.J.: Glencoe Press, 1969.

78. Bosworth, Allan R. AMERICA'S CONCENTRATION CAMPS. New York, N.Y.: W. W. Norton Co., 1967.

79. Bradt, Acken G. THE SECRETS OF GETTING RESULTS THROUGH PEOPLE. Englewood Cliffs, N.J.: Prentice Hall, 1967,

80. Breckenridge, Adam. THE RIGHT TO PRIVACY. Lincoln, Neb.:
     University of Nebraska, 1970.

81. Breitman, George. THE LAST YEAR OF MALCOLM X: THE
     EVOLUTION OF A REVOLUTIONARY. New York, N.Y.:
     Pathfinder Press, 1967.

82. Brink, William. BLACK AND WHITE. New York, N.Y.: Simon and
     Schuster, 1967.

83. Brody, Eugene B. MINORITY GROUP ADOLESCENTS IN THE
     UNITED STATES. Baltimore, Md.: Williams and Wilkins, 1968.

84. Brotz, Howard M. THE BLACK JEWS OF HARLEM: NEGRO
     NATIONALISM AND THE DILEMMAS OF NEGRO LEADER-
     SHIP. New York, N.Y.: Schocken Books, 1970.

85. Brown, Michael. THE POLITICS AND ANTI-POLITICS OF THE
     YOUNG. Riverside, N.J.: Glencoe Press, 1969.

86. Bull, Norman J. MORAL JUDGMENT FROM CHILDHOOD TO
     ADOLESCENCE. Beverly Hills, Calif.: Sage Publications, 1970.

87. Bullock, Charles, and Harrell R. Rodgers (eds.). BLACK POLITICAL
     ATTITUDES: IMPLICATIONS FOR POLITICAL SUPPORT.
     Chicago, Ill.: Markham, 1972.

88. Burris, Donald S. THE RIGHT TO TREATMENT. New York, N.Y.:
     Springer Publishing Co., 1969.

89. Burton, Lindy. VULNERABLE CHILDREN—THREE STUDIES OF
     CHILDREN IN CONFLICT: ACCIDENT INVOLVED CHILDREN,
     SEXUALLY ASSAULTED CHILDREN AND CHILDREN WITH
     ASTHMA. New York, N.Y.: Schocken Books, 1968.

90. Caffi, Andrea. A CRITIQUE OF VIOLENCE. Indianapolis, Ind.:
     Bobbs-Merrill, 1969.

91. Campbell, Alan (ed.). THE STATES AND THE URBAN CRISIS.
     Englewood Cliffs, N.J.: Prentice Hall, 1970.

92. Campbell, Angus. WHITE ATTITUDES TOWARD BLACK PEOPLE.
     Ann Arbor, Mich.: University of Michigan, 1971.

★   93. Campbell, James S., and others (eds.). LAW AND ORDER
     RECONSIDERED: A STAFF REPORT TO THE NATIONAL
     COMMISSION ON THE CAUSES AND PREVENTION OF
     VIOLENCE. New York, N.Y.: Praeger Publishers, 1971.

94. Cantril, Albert, and Charles W. Roll. HOPES AND FEARS OF THE AMERICAN PEOPLE. New York, N.Y.: Universe Books, 1971.

95. Canty, Donald. A SINGLE SOCIETY: ALTERNATIVES TO URBAN APARTHEID. New York, N.Y.: Praeger Publishers, 1969.

96. Capaldi, Nicholas (ed.). CLEAR AND PRESENT DANGER: THE FREE SPEECH CONTROVERSY. New York, N.Y.: Pegasus, 1970.

97. Caplan, Gerald, and Serge Lebovici. ADOLESCENCE: PSYCHO-SOCIAL PERSPECTIVES. Scranton, Pa.: Basic Books, 1969.

★ 98. Carmichael, Stokely, and Charles V. Hamilton. BLACK POWER: THE POLITICS OF LIBERATION IN AMERICA. Westminster, Md.: Random House, 1968.

99. Cartwright, Dorwin, and Alvin Zander. GROUP DYNAMICS, RESEARCH AND THEORY. New York, N.Y.: Harper and Row, 1968.

100. Cavan, Ruth Shonle. THE AMERICAN FAMILY. New York, N.Y.: Thomas Y. Crowell Co., 1969.

101. Chametzky, Jules, and Sidney Kaplan. BLACK AND WHITE IN AMERICAN CULTURE: AN ANTHOLOGY FROM THE MASSACHUSETTS REVIEW. Amherst, Mass.: University of Massachusetts Press, 1969.

102. Chapman, Brian. POLICE STATE. New York, N.Y.: Praeger, 1970.

103. Christensen, Barlow. LAWYERS FOR PEOPLE OF MODERATE MEANS, SOME PROBLEMS OF AVAILABILITY OF LEGAL SERVICES. Chicago, Ill.: American Bar Foundation, 1970.

104. Clark, Kenneth. PSYCHOLOGY. Englewood Cliffs, N.J.: Prentice Hall, 1970.

105. Clark, Terry. COMMUNITY STRUCTURE AND DECISION-MAKING: COMPARATIVE ANALYSES. San Francisco, Calif.: Chandler Publishing Co., 1968.

★ 106. Clinard, Marshall B. SOCIOLOGY OF DEVIANT BEHAVIOR. New York, N.Y.: Holt, Rinehart and Winston, 1968.

107. Cohen, Carl. CIVIL DISOBEDIENCE: CONSCIENCE, TACTICS, AND THE LAW. Irvington, N.Y.: Columbia University Press, 1971.

108. Cole, Larry. STREET KIDS. New York, N.Y.: Grossman Publishing Co., 1970.

109. Comstock, Anthony. TRAPS FOR THE YOUNG. Cambridge, Mass.: Harvard University Press, 1967.

★ 110. Conant, Ralph W., and Molly Apple Levin (eds.). PROBLEMS IN RESEARCH ON COMMUNITY VIOLENCE. New York, N.Y.: Praeger Publishers, 1969.

111. Conant, Ralph W. THE PROSPECTS FOR REVOLUTION: A STUDY OF RIOTS, CIVIL DISOBEDIENCE, AND INSURRECTION IN CONTEMPORARY AMERICA. New York, N.Y.: Harper and Row, 1971.

112. Conot, Robert. RIVERS OF BLOOD, YEARS OF DARKNESS: THE UNFORGETTABLE CLASSIC ACCOUNT OF THE WATTS RIOT. West Caldwell, N.J.: William Morrow and Co., 1968.

113. Conrad, Earl. THE INVENTION OF THE NEGRO. New York, N.Y.: Paul S. Eriksson, 1969.

114. Coser, Lewis A. CONTINUITIES IN THE STUDY OF SOCIAL CONFLICT. New York, N.Y.: Free Press, 1967.

115. CRIME AND PRESIDENTIAL COMMISSIONS. (Cassette tape, 53 min.) North Hollywood, Calif.: Center for Cassette Studies.

116. Cruse, Harold. THE CRISIS OF THE NEGRO INTELLECTUAL. West Caldwell, N.J.: William Morrow and Co., 1967.

117. Cumming, Elaine. SYSTEMS OF SOCIAL REGULATION. Chicago, Ill.: Aldine/Atherton, 1968.

118. Daniels, David N., and others. VIOLENCE AND THE STRUGGLE FOR EXISTENCE. Waltham, Mass.: Little Brown and Co., 1970.

119. Davis, F. James. SOCIAL PROBLEMS. Riverside, N.J.: Free Press, 1970.

120. Davis, Keith. HUMAN RELATIONS AT WORK. New York, N.Y.: McGraw-Hill, 1967.

121. Davis, Kenneth Culp. DISCRETIONARY JUSTICE: A PRELIMINARY INQUIRY. Baton Rouge, La.: Louisiana State University Press, 1969.

122. DeMaris, Ovid. AMERICA THE VIOLENT. New York, N.Y.: Cowles Book Co., 1970.

★ 123. DeMaris, Ovid. CAPTIVE CITY. Englewood Cliffs, N.J.: Prentice Hall, 1970.

124. Demerath, N. J., and R. Peterson. SYSTEM, CHANGE, AND CONFLICT. New York, N.Y.: Free Press, 1967.

125. Dentler, Robert A., Bernard Mackler, and Mary Ellen Warshauser. URBAN R's: RACE RELATIONS AS THE PROBLEM IN URBAN EDUCATION. New York, N.Y.: Praeger Publishers, 1967.

126. Denzin, Norman. SOCIOLOGICAL METHODS: A SOURCEBOOK. Chicago, Ill.: Aldine/Atherton, 1970.

127. Donaldson, Scott. THE SUBURBAN MYTH. Irvington, N.Y.: Columbia University Press, 1969.

128. Donovan, Frank R. RAISING YOUR CHILDREN: WHAT BEHAVIORAL SCIENTISTS HAVE DISCOVERED. New York, N.Y.: Thomas Y. Crowell Co., 1968.

129. Donovan, Frank R. WILD KIDS: HOW YOUTH HAS SHOCKED ITS ELDERS—THEN AND NOW! Harrisburg, Pa.: Stackpole Co., 1967.

130. Douglas, Jack D. AMERICAN SOCIAL ORDER. Riverside, N.J.: Free Press, 1971.

131. Douglas, Jack D. DEVIANCE & RESPECTABILITY: THE SOCIAL CONSTRUCTION OF MORAL MEANINGS. New York, N.Y.: Basic Books, 1970.

132. Douglas, Jack D. YOUTH IN TURMOIL: AMERICA'S CHANGING YOUTH CULTURES AND STUDENT PROTEST MOVEMENTS. U.S. Center for Studies of Crime and Delinquency, National Institute of Mental Health. Washington, D.C.: U.S. Government Printing Office, 1970.

133. Downs, Anthony. URBAN PROBLEMS AND PROSPECTS. Chicago, Ill.: Markham Publishing, 1970.

134. Drotning, Phillip T., and Wesley Smith. UP FROM THE GHETTO. New York, N.Y.: Cowles Book Co., 1969.

★ 135. Drucker, Peter F. THE AGE OF DISCONTINUITY: GUIDELINES TO OUR CHANGING SOCIETY. New York, N.Y.: Harper and Row, 1969.

136. Dye, Thomas. POLITICS IN STATES AND COMMUNITIES. Englewood Cliffs, N.J.: Prentice Hall, 1969.

137. Dynes, Russel R. ORGANIZED BEHAVIOR IN DISASTER. Lexington, Mass.: Lexington Books, 1970.

138. Eldredge, H. Wentworth. TAMING MEGALOPOLIS (2 vols.). Garden City, N.Y.: Doubleday and Co., 1967.

139. Ellis, William W. WHITE ETHICS AND BLACK POWER: THE EMERGENCE OF THE WEST SIDE ORGANIZATION. Chicago, Ill.: Aldine/Atherton, 1969.

140. THE END OF PRIVACY. (Cassette tape, 28 min.) North Hollywood, Calif.: Center for Cassette Studies.

★ 141. Endleman, Shalom (ed.). VIOLENCE IN THE STREETS. Chicago, Ill.: Quadrangle Books, 1970.

142. Epstein, C. INTERGROUP RELATIONS FOR POLICE OFFICERS. New York, N.Y.: Hafner Publishing Co., 1970.

143. Erickson, Eric H. IDENTITY: YOUTH AND CRISIS. New York, N.Y.: W. W. Norton and Co., 1968.

144. Etzkowitz, Henry, and Gerald Schaflander. GHETTO CRISIS: RIOTS OR RECONCILIATION. Waltham, Mass.: Little Brown and Co., 1969.

145. Ewald, William R., Jr. (ed.). ENVIRONMENT FOR MAN: THE NEXT FIFTY YEARS. Bloomington, Ind.: Indiana University Press, 1967.

146. Faas, Larry A. THE EMOTIONALLY DISTURBED CHILD: A BOOK OF READINGS. Springfield, Ill.: Charles C. Thomas, 1970.

147. Flammang, C. J. THE POLICE AND THE UNDERPROTECTED CHILDREN. Springfield, Ill.: Charles C. Thomas, 1970.

148. Foner, Philip S. THE BLACK PANTHERS SPEAK. Philadelphia, Pa.: J. B. Lippincott Co., 1970.

149. Forer, Lois G. "NO ONE WILL LISSEN": HOW OUR LEGAL SYSTEM BRUTALIZES THE YOUTHFUL POOR. Scranton, Pa.: John Day Co., 1970.

150. Fortune, Editors. THE NEGRO AND THE CITY. Morristown, N.J.: Time-Life, 1968.

151. Fortune, Monte, and Robert Heyer. AM I A RACIST. New York, N.Y.: Association Press, 1969.

152. Franklin, John Hope. COLOR AND RACE. Boston, Mass.: Beacon Press, 1969.

153. Frazier, Edward Franklin. NEGRO YOUTH AT THE CROSSWAYS: THEIR PERSONALITY DEVELOPMENT IN THE MIDDLE STATES. New York, N.Y.: Schocken Books, 1967.

154. Freedman, Jonathan L., and Anthony Doob. DEVIANCY: THE PSYCHOLOGY OF BEING DIFFERENT. New York, N.Y.: Academic Press, 1968.

155. Freeman, Howard E., and Norman Kurtz (eds.). AMERICA'S TROUBLES. Englewood Cliffs, N.J.: Prentice Hall, 1973.

156. Friedman, Murray, and others. OVERCOMING MIDDLE CLASS RAGE. Philadelphia, Pa.: Westminster Press, 1971.

157. Fritschler, A. L. SMOKING AND POLITICS, POLICYMAKING AND THE FEDERAL BUREAUCRACY. New York, N.Y.: Appleton-Century-Crofts, 1969.

158. Galbraith, John Kenneth. THE AFFLUENT SOCIETY. Burlington, Mass.: Houghton Mifflin Co., 1971.

159. Gallagher, Robert S. "IF I HAD IT TO DO OVER AGAIN...": AMERICA'S ADULT DROPOUTS. New York, N.Y.: E. P. Dutton and Co., 1969.

160. Garn, Stanley M. HUMAN RACES. Springfield, Ill.: Charles C. Thomas, 1971.

161. Ganz, Alan S., and others. THE CITIES AND THE POLICE. Chicago, Ill.: University of Chicago Press, 1968.

162. Glaser, Daniel. SOCIAL DEVIANCE. Chicago, Ill.: Markham Publishing Co., 1971.

163. Glasrud, Bruce, and Alan M. Smith. PROMISES TO KEEP. Chicago, Ill.: Rand McNally, 1972.

164. Glazer, Nathan, and Daniel P. Moynihan. BEYOND THE MELTING POT: THE NEGROES, PUERTO RICANS, JEWS, ITALIANS, AND IRISH OF NEW YORK CITY. Cambridge, Mass.: Massachusetts Institute Technology Press, 1970.

★ 165. Glazer, Nathan. CITIES IN TROUBLE. Chicago, Ill.: Quadrangle Books, 1970.

166. Glessing, Robert J. THE UNDERGROUND PRESS IN AMERICA. Bloomington, Ind.: Indiana University Press, 1970.

167. Glock, Charles, and Ellen Siegelman. PREJUDICE U.S.A. New York, N.Y.: Praeger Publishers, 1969.

★ 168. Gold, Harry, and Frank R. Scarpitti. COMBATTING SOCIAL PROBLEMS: TECHNIQUES OF INTERVENTION. New York, N.Y.: Holt Rinehart and Winston, 1967.

169. Gold, Martin. DELINQUENT BEHAVIOR IN AN AMERICAN CITY. Monterey, Calif.: Brooks-Cole Publishing Co., 1972.

170. Graham, Hugh Davis. VIOLENCE IN AMERICA: HISTORICAL AND COMPARATIVE PERSPECTIVES. New York, N.Y.: Praeger Publishers, 1969.

171. Green, Constance. THE SECRET CITY: A HISTORY OF RACE RELATIONS IN THE NATION'S CAPITAL. Princeton, N.J.: Princeton University Press, 1967.

172. Greenberg, Harold. SOCIAL ENVIRONMENT AND BEHAVIOR. Cambridge, Mass.: Schenkman Publishing Co., 1970.

173. Grier, William H., and Price M. Cobbs. BLACK RAGE. New York, N.Y.: Basic Books, 1968.

★ 174. Grimshaw, Allen D. RACIAL VIOLENCE IN THE UNITED STATES. Chicago, Ill.: Aldine/Atherton, 1969.

175. Griswold, H. Jack. AN EYE FOR AN EYE. New York, N.Y.: Holt Rinehart and Winston, 1970.

176. Haddad, William F., and G. Douglas Pugh (eds.). BLACK ECONOMIC DEVELOPMENT. Englewood Cliffs, N.J.: Prentice Hall, 1969.

177. Hadden, Jeffrey K., and others. A TIME TO BURN: A CRITICAL EVALUATION OF THE PRESENT AMERICAN RACE RELATIONS CRISIS. Chicago, Ill.: Rand McNally, 1969.

178. Hall, Calvin S., and Gardner Lindzey. THEORIES OF PERSONALITY. New York, N.Y.: John Wiley and Sons, 1970.

179. Hall, Robert E. (ed.). ABORTION IN A CHANGING WORLD (2 vols.).Irvington, N.Y.: Columbia University Press, 1970.

180. Hammer, Richard. BETWEEN LIFE AND DEATH. Riverside, N.J.: Macmillan Co., 1969.

181. Hannerz, Ulf. SOULSIDE: INQUIRIES INTO GHETTO CULTURE AND COMMUNITY. Irvington, N.Y.: Columbia University Press, 1969.

182. Harris, Fred, and John V. Lindsey. STATE OF THE CITIES: REPORT OF THE COMMISSION ON CITIES IN THE 70's. New York, N.Y.: Praeger Publishers, 1972.

183. Harris, Richard. JUSTICE: THE CRISIS OF LAW, ORDER AND FREEDOM IN AMERICA. New York, N.Y.: E. P. Dutton Co., 1970.

★ 184. Harris, Richard. THE FEAR OF CRIME. New York, N.Y.: Praeger Publishers, 1969.

★ 185. Hartogs, Renatus, and Eric Artst. VIOLENCE: CAUSES AND SOL-UTIONS. New York, N.Y.: Dell Publishing Co., 1970.

186. Hauser, Stuart. BLACK AND WHITE IDENTITY FORMATION: EXPLORATIONS IN THE PSYCHO-SOCIAL DEVELOPMENT OF WHITE AND NEGRO MALE ADOLESCENTS. New York, N.Y.: Wiley-Interstate, 1971.

187. Haveman, Robert, and Julius Margolis. PUBLIC EXPENDITURES AND POLICY ANALYSIS. Chicago, Ill.: Markham Publishing Co., 1970.

188. Hayden, Tom. REBELLION AND REPRESSION. Cleveland, Ohio: World Publishing Co., 1969.

189. Hentoff, Nat (ed.). BLACK ANTI-SEMITISM AND JEWISH RACISM. New York, N.Y.: R. W. Baron Co., 1969.

190. Hernandez, Luis F. THE FORGOTTEN AMERICAN. Philadelphia, Pa.: Anti-Defamation League, 1969.

191. Hess, Robert D., and Judith V. Torney. THE DEVELOPMENT OF POLITICAL ATTITUDES IN CHILDREN. Garden City, N.Y.: Doubleday and Co., 1968.

192. Hewitt, John P. SOCIAL STRATIFICATION AND DEVIANT BEHAVIOR. Westminster, Md.: Random House, 1970.

193. Hoffman, Martin. THE GAY WORLD: MALE HOMOSEXUALITY AND THE SOCIAL CREATION OF EVIL. New York, N.Y.: Basic Books, 1968.

★ 194. Hofstadter, Richard, and Michael Wallace. AMERICAN VIOLENCE: A DOCUMENTARY HISTORY. New York, N.Y.: Alfred A. Knopf, 1970.

195. Holleb, Doris B. SOCIAL AND ECONOMIC INFORMATION FOR URBAN PLANNING. Chicago, Ill.: University of Chicago, 1969.

196. Hook, Sidney. ACADEMIC FREEDOM AND ACADEMIC ANARCHY. New York, N.Y.: Cowles Book Co., 1970.

197. Hoover, J. Edgar. COMMUNISM. Westminster, Md.: Random House, 1969.

198. Hough, Joseph C., Jr. BLACK POWER AND WHITE PROTESTANTS: A CHRISTIAN RESPONSE TO THE NEW NEGRO PLURALISM. New York, N.Y.: Oxford University Press, 1968.

199. Houts, Marshall. THEY ASKED FOR DEATH. Chicago, Ill.: Cowles Book Co., 1970.

200. Howe, Frederic. THE CITY, THE HOPE OF DEMOCRACY. Seattle, Wash.: University of Washington Press, 1969.

201. HUNGER. (Cassette tape, 22 min.) North Hollywood, Calif.: Center for Cassette Studies.

202. Hutchinson, John. THE IMPERFECT UNION: CORRUPTION IN AMERICAN TRADE UNIONS. New York, N.Y.: E. P. Dutton, 1972.

203. IS IT ALWAYS RIGHT TO BE RIGHT. (16mm color, 8 min.) Malibu, Calif.: Stephen Bosustow Productions.

★ 204. Isenberg, Irwin (comp.). THE CITY IN CRISIS. New York, N.Y.: H. W. Wilson, 1968.

205. Jacobs, Jane. THE ECONOMY OF CITIES. Westminster, Md.: Random House, 1970.

206.   Jacobs, Jerry. ADOLESCENT SUICIDE. New York, N.Y.: John Wiley and Sons, 1970.

207.   Jacobs, Paul. PRELUDE TO RIOT: A VIEW OF AMERICA FROM THE BOTTOM. Westminster, Md.: Random House, 1968.

★ 208.   James, Howard. CHILDREN IN TROUBLE: A NATIONAL SCAN-DAL. New York, N.Y.: David McKay Co., 1970.

209.   Jay, Anthony. THE NEW ORATORY. Riverside, N.J.: Macmillan Co., 1971.

210.   Jessor, Richard, and others. SOCIETY, PERSONALITY, AND DEVIANT BEHAVIOR: A STUDY OF A TRI-ETHNIC COMMUN-ITY. New York, N.Y.: Holt Rinehart and Winston, 1968.

211.   Jones, James. PREJUDICE AND RACISM. Reading, Mass.: Addison-Wesley, 1972.

212.   Justice, Blair. ASSESSING POTENTIALS FOR RACIAL VIO-LENCE. Houston, Texas: Rice University, 1968.

213.   Justice, Blair. EFFECTS OF RACIAL VIOLENCE ON ATTITUDES IN THE NEGRO COMMUNITY. Houston, Texas: Rice University, 1968.

214.   Justice, Blair. VIOLENCE IN THE CITY. Fort Worth, Texas: Texas Christian University Press, 1969.

215.   Kahn, S. HOW PEOPLE GET POWER ORGANIZING OPPRESSED COMMUNITIES FOR ACTION. New York, N.Y.: McGraw-Hill, 1970.

216   Kalish, Richard A. THE PSYCHOLOGY OF HUMAN BEHAVIOR. Monterey, Calif.: Brooks-Cole Publishing Co., 1972.

217   Katz, William L. EYEWITNESS: THE NEGRO IN AMERICAN HISTORY. New York, N.Y.: Pitman Publishing Corp., 1971.

218.   Kavolis, Vytautas. COMPARATIVE PERSPECTIVES ON SOCIAL PROBLEMS. Boston, Mass.: Little, Brown and Co., 1969.

219.   Keniston, Kenneth. YOUNG RADICALS: NOTES ON COMMITTED YOUTH. New York, N.Y.: Harcourt, Brace & World, 1968.

220.   Klein, M. W. STREET GANGS AND STREET WORKERS. Engle-wood Cliffs, N.J.: Prentice Hall, 1971.

★ 221. Killian, Lewis M. THE IMPOSSIBLE REVOLUTION: BLACK POWER AND THE AMERICAN DREAM. Westminster, Md.: Random House, 1968.

222. King, Martin Luther, Jr. WHERE DO WE GO FROM HERE: CHAOS OR COMMUNITY. New York, N.Y.: Harper and Row, 1967.

223. Kirkham, James F. ASSASSINATION AND POLITICAL VIOLENCE. New York, N.Y.: Praeger Publishers, 1970.

224. Knowles, Louis, and Kenneth Prewitt. INSTITUTIONAL RACISM IN AMERICA. Englewood Cliffs, N.J.: Prentice Hall, 1969.

225. Kuhn, Thomas S. THE STRUCTURE OF SCIENTIFIC REVOLU- TIONS. Chicago, Ill., University of Chicago Press, 1970.

226. Knudten, Richard D. THE CHRISTIAN ENCOUNTERS CRIME IN AMERICAN SOCIETY. St. Louis, Mo.: Concordia Publishing House, 1969.

227. Labby, Daniel H. LIFE OR DEATH: ETHICS AND OPTIONS. Seattle, Wash.: University of Washington Press, 1968.

228. Landis, Judson R. CURRENT PERSPECTIVES ON SOCIAL PROB- LEMS. Belmont, Calif.: Wadsworth Publishing Co., 1969.

229. Lane, Mark. CHICAGO EYEWITNESS. Stamford, Conn.: Astor- Honor, 1968.

230. Larsen, Otto N. (ed.). VIOLENCE AND THE MASS MEDIA. New York, N.Y.: Harper and Row, 1968.

231. Larson, Orvin. WHEN IT'S YOUR TURN TO SPEAK. New York, N.Y.: Harper and Row, 1971.

232. Lazarsfeld, Paul, William Sewell, and Harold Wilensky (eds.). THE USES OF SOCIOLOGY. New York, N.Y.: Basic Books, 1967.

233. Lecky, Robert S., and Elliott H. Wright. BLACK MANIFESTO: RELIGION, RACISM AND REPARATION. New York, N.Y.: Sheed and Ward, 1969.

234. Leggett, John C. CLASS, RACE, AND LABOR: WORKING-CLASS CONSCIOUSNESS IN DETROIT. New York, N.Y.: Oxford Univer- sity Press, 1971.

235. Leinwand, Gerald. THE CITY AS A COMMUNITY. New York, N.Y.: Simon and Schuster, 1970.

236.   Lemert, Edwin M. HUMAN DEVIANCE: SOCIAL PROBLEMS AND SOCIAL CONTROL. Englewood Cliffs, N.J.: Prentice Hall, 1967.

★ 237.   Liebow, Eliot. TALLY'S CORNER. Boston, Mass.: Little, Brown and Co., 1967.

238.   Lifton, Robert Jay. HISTORY AND HUMAN SURVIVAL. Westminster, Md.: Random House, 1971.

239.   Lindesmith, Alfred R., and Anselm L. Strauss. SOCIAL PSYCHOLOGY. New York, N.Y.: Holt Rinehart and Winston, 1968.

240.   Lindesmith, Alfred R., and Anselm L. Strauss (eds.). READINGS IN SOCIAL PSYCHOLOGY. New York, N.Y.: Holt Rinehart and Winston, 1969.

★ 241.   Lipsky, Michael (ed.). LAW AND ORDER: POLICE ENCOUNTERS. Chicago, Ill.: Aldine/Atherton, 1970.

242.   Lofland, John. DEVIANCE AND IDENTITY. Englewood Cliffs, N.J.: Prentice Hall, 1969.

243.   Love, Harold D. THE EMOTIONALLY DISTURBED CHILD: A PARENT'S GUIDE FOR PARENTS WHO HAVE PROBLEM CHILDREN. Springfield, Ill.: Charles C. Thomas, 1970.

244.   Lowe, David. KU KLUX KLAN: THE INVISIBLE EMPIRE. New York, N.Y.: W. W. Norton and Co., 1967.

245.   Mack, Raymond W. PREJUDICE AND RACE RELATIONS. Chicago, Ill.: Quadrangle Books, 1970.

★ 246.   Mack, Raymond W. RACE, CLASS, AND POWER. Cincinnati, Ohio: Van Nostrand Reinhold Co., 1968.

247.   McNeil, Elton B. THE QUIET FURIES: DISORDERS AND MAN. Englewood Cliffs, N.J.: Prentice Hall, 1968.

248.   Margolius, Sidney. YOUR PERSONAL GUIDE TO SUCCESSFUL RETIREMENT. Westminster, Md.: Random House, 1969.

249.   Martin, James, and Adrian Norman. THE COMPUTERIZED SOCIETY. Englewood Cliffs, N.J.: Prentice Hall, 1970.

250.   Marx, Gary T. PROTEST AND PREJUDICE. New York, N.Y.: Harper and Row, 1967.

251. Mason, Philip. RACE RELATIONS. New York, N.Y.: Oxford University Press, 1970.

252. Matza, David. BECOMING DEVIANT. Engelwood Cliffs, N.J.: Prentice Hall, 1969.

253. McCone, J. A. VIOLENCE IN THE CITY: AN END OR A BEGINNING. Los Angeles, Calif.: Lucas Brothers, 1970.

★ 254. McCord, William, and others. LIFE STYLES IN THE BLACK GHETTO. New York, N.Y.: W. W. Norton and Co., 1969.

★ 255. McIntyre, Donald M., Jr. (ed.). LAW ENFORCEMENT IN THE METROPOLIS: A WORKING PAPER ON THE CRIMINAL LAW SYSTEM IN DETROIT. Chicago, Ill.: American Bar Foundation, 1967.

256. Mead, Margaret. CULTURE AND COMMITMENT. New York, N.Y.: Doubleday and Co., 1970.

257. Megargee, Edwin I. THE DYNAMICS OF AGGRESSION: INDIVIDUAL, GROUP, AND INTERNATIONAL ANALYSES. New York, N.Y.: Harper and Row, 1970.

258. Meir, August (ed.). BLACK EXPERIENCE: THE TRANSFORMATION OF ACTIVISM. Chicago, Ill.: Aldine/Atherton, 1970.

★ 259. Merton, Robert K., and Robert Nisbet. CONTEMPORARY SOCIAL PROBLEMS. New York, N.Y.: Harcourt Brace Jovanovich, 1971.

260. Merton, Robert K. SOCIAL THEORY AND SOCIAL STRUCTURE. Riverside, N.J.: Free Press, 1968.

261. Miller, Arthur. THE ASSAULT ON PRIVACY: COMPUTERS, DATA BANKS AND DOSSIERS. Ann Arbor, Mich.: University of Michigan, 1971.

262. Miller, Kelly. RADICALS AND CONSERVATIVES AND OTHER ESSAYS ON THE NEGRO IN AMERICA. New York, N.Y.: Schocken Books, 1968.

263. MINORITIES AS MAJORITIES. (Cassette tape, 55 min.) North Hollywood, Calif.: Center for Cassette Studies.

264. Mintz, Morton, and Jerry Cohen. AMERICA INC.—WHO OWNS AND OPERATES THE UNITED STATES. New York, N.Y.: Dial Press, 1971.

30   BEHAVIORAL AND SOCIAL SCIENCES

265. Mitau, G. Theodore. DECADE OF DECISION: THE SUPREME
      COURT AND THE CONSTITUTIONAL REVOLUTION. New York,
      N.Y.: Charles Scribner's Sons, 1968.

266. Moore, William, Jr. THE VERTICAL GHETTO: EVERYDAY LIFE
      IN AN URBAN PROJECT. Westminster, Md.: Random House, 1968.

267. Moreland, Lois. WHITE RACISM AND THE LAW. Columbus, Ohio:
      C. E. Merrill, 1970.

268. Mosher, Frederick. DEMOCRACY AND THE PUBLIC SERVICE. New
      York, N.Y.: Oxford University Press, 1968.

269. Moskow, Michael H. COLLECTIVE BARGAINING IN PUBLIC
      EMPLOYMENT. Westminster, Md.: Random House, 1970.

★ 270. Moynihan, Daniel. MAXIMUM FEASIBLE MISUNDERSTANDING.
      New York, N.Y.: Free Press, 1969.

271. Moynihan, Daniel P. (ed.). TOWARD A NATIONAL URBAN
      POLICY. New York, N.Y.: Basic Books, 1970.

★ 272. Muse, Benjamin. THE AMERICAN NEGRO REVOLUTION FROM
      NON-VIOLENCE TO BLACK POWER. Bloomington, Ind.:
      Indiana University Press, 1968.

273. National Federation of Settlements and Neighborhood Centers.
      NEIGHBORHOOD GANGS: A CASE BOOK FOR YOUTH
      WORKERS. New York, N.Y.: National Federation of Settlements
      and Neighborhood Centers, 1967.

274. THE NATURE OF PREJUDICE. (Sound filmstrip, color.) Gaithers-
      burg, Md.: International Association of Chiefs of Police.

★ 275. Niederhoffer, Arthur. THE AMBIVALENT FORCE: PERSPECTIVES
      ON THE POLICE. Waltham, Mass.: Ginn & Co., 1970.

276. Nisbet, Robert A. THE SOCIAL BOND. New York, N.Y.: Alfred A.
      Knopf, 1970.

277. Oppenheimer, Martin. THE URBAN GUERRILLA. Cleveland, Ohio:
      Quadrangle Books, 1969.

278. Pascal, Anthony (ed.). RACIAL DISCRIMINATION IN ECONOMIC
      LIFE. Lexington, Mass.: Lexington Books, 1972.

279. Perloff, Harvey. THE FUTURE OF THE UNITED STATES
      GOVERNMENT: TOWARD THE YEAR 2000. New York, N.Y.:
      George Braziller, 1971.

280. Pivan, Frances, and Richard Cloward. REGULATING THE POOR: THE FUNCTIONS OF PUBLIC RELIEF. Westminster, Md.: Random House, 1972.

281. Potter, John Deane. THE ART OF HANGING. Cranberry, N.J.: A. S. Barnes and Co., 1969.

282. POVERTY IS BLACK AND WHITE. (Cassette tape, 27 min.) North Hollywood, Calif.: Center for Cassette Studies.

283. Rabkin, Leslie Y. SOURCEBOOK IN ABNORMAL PSYCHOLOGY. Boston, Mass.: Houghton Mifflin, 1967.

284. Reciss, Henry. REVENUE SHARING: CRUTCH OR CATALYST FOR STATE AND LOCAL GOVERNMENTS. New York, N.Y.: Praeger Publishers, 1970.

285. Reeves, Herman. CONSUMER PROTECTION IN THE STATES. Lexington, Ky.: Council of State Governments, 1970.

286. THE RENEWAL OF OUR CITIES. (Cassette tape, 25 min.) North Hollywood, Calif.: Center for Cassette Studies.

287. Reynolds, G. Scott. THE MORTALITY MERCHANTS. New York, N.Y.: David McKay, 1968.

288. Rivlin, Alice. SYSTEMATIC THINKING FOR SOCIAL ACTION. Washington, D.C.: Brookings Institute, 1971.

289. Romm, Ethel. THE OPEN CONSPIRACY: WHAT AMERICA'S ANGRY GENERATION IS SAYING. Harrisburg, Pa.: Stackpole, 1970.

290. Rose, Gordon. SCHOOLS FOR YOUNG OFFENDERS. New York, N.Y.: Barnes and Noble, 1967.

291. Rose, Peter I. (ed.). THE STUDY OF SOCIETY—AN INTEGRATED ANTHOLOGY. Westminster, Md.: Random House, 1970.

292. Rose, Peter Isaac. THE SUBJECT IS RACE: TRADITIONAL IDEOLOGIES AND THE TEACHING OF RACE RELATIONS. New York, N.Y.: Oxford University Press, 1968.

293. Rose, Thomas (ed.). VIOLENCE IN AMERICA: A HISTORICAL AND CONTEMPORARY READER. Westminster, Md.: Random House, 1969.

294. Rothman, David. THE DISCOVERY OF THE ASYLUM-SOCIAL ORDER AND DISORDER IN THE NEW REPUBLIC. Waltham, Mass.: Little, Brown and Co., 1972.

295. Rubington, Earl, and Martin S. Weinberg (eds.). DEVIANCE: THE INTERACTIONIST PERSPECTIVE. New York, N.Y.: Macmillan Co., 1968.

296. Sagarin, Edward. ODD MAN IN: SOCIETIES OF DEVIANTS IN AMERICA. Cleveland, Ohio: Quadrangle Books, 1969.

297. Sagarin, Edward, and Donald MacNamara (eds.). PROBLEMS OF SEX BEHAVIOR. New York, N.Y.: Thomas Y. Crowell Co., 1968.

298. Schacter, Stanley. EMOTION, OBESITY AND CRIME. New York, N.Y.: Academic Press, 1971.

299. Schaefer, Walter V. THE SUSPECT AND SOCIETY: CRIMINAL PROCEDURE AND CONVERGING CONSTITUTIONAL DOC-TRINES. Evanston, Ill.: Northwestern University Press, 1967.

300. Schafer, Stephen. COMPENSATION AND RESTITUTION TO VICTIMS OF CRIME. Montclair, N.J.: Patterson-Smith, 1970.

301. Scheuer, James. TO WALK THE STREETS SAFELY. Garden City, N.Y.: Doubleday and Co., 1969.

★ 302. Schlesinger, Arthur M., Jr. THE CRISIS OF CONFIDENCE: IDEAS, POWER AND VIOLENCE IN AMERICA. Burlington, Mass.: Houghton-Mifflin, 1969.

303. SCHOOLS AND EQUALITY. (Cassette tape, 23 min.) North Hollywood, Calif.: Center for Cassette Studies.

304. Schuchter, Arnold. WHITE POWER/BLACK FREEDOM. Boston, Mass.: Beacon Press, 1969.

305. Schultz, David A. COMING UP BLACK: PATTERNS OF GHETTO SOCIALIZATION. Englewood Cliffs, N.J.: Prentice Hall, 1969.

306. Schur, Edwin M. LAW AND SOCIETY: A SOCIOLOGICAL VIEW. Westminster, Md.: Random House, 1967.

307. Scott, James. COMPARATIVE POLITICAL CORRUPTION. Englewood Cliffs, N.J.: Prentice Hall, 1972.

308. Segal, Ronald. THE RACE WAR. New York, N.Y.: Viking Press, 1967.

309. Seligman, Ben B. PERMANENT POVERTY: AN AMERICAN SYNDROME. Cleveland, Ohio: Quadrangle Books, 1968.

310. Selznick, Gertrude J. THE TENACITY OF PREJUDICE: ANTI-SEMITISM IN CONTEMPORARY AMERICA. New York, N.Y.: Harper and Row, 1969.

311. Sennett, Richard. THE USES OF DISORDER: PERSONAL IDEN-TITY AND CITY LIFE. Westminster, Md.: Random House, 1971.

312. Servin, Manuel. THE MEXICAN-AMERICANS: AN AWAKENING MINORITY. Riverside, N.J.: Glencoe Press, 1970.

313. Shank, Alan (ed.). POLITICAL POWER AND THE URBAN CRISIS. Boston, Mass.: Holbrook Press, 1973.

314. Sharkansky, Ira. THE POLITICS OF TAXING AND SPENDING. Indianapolis, Ind.: Bobbs-Merrill, 1969.

315. Skinner, B. F. BEYOND FREEDOM AND DIGNITY. New York, N.Y.: Alfred A. Knopf, 1971.

316. Skolnick, Jerome, and Elliot Currie. CRISIS IN AMERICAN INSTI-TUTIONS. Waltham, Mass.: Little, Brown and Co., 1970.

317. Skolnick, Jerome H. THE POLITICS OF PROTEST. New York, N.Y.: Simon and Schuster, 1969.

318. Slough, M. C. PRIVACY, FREEDOM AND RESPONSIBILITY. Springfield, Ill.: Charles C. Thomas, 1969.

319. Smelser, Neil, and William T. Smelser. PERSONALITY AND SOCIAL SYSTEMS. New York, N.Y.: John Wiley and Sons, 1970.

320. Smith, Alexander, and Harriet Pollack. CRIME AND JUSTICE IN A MASS SOCIETY. Lexington, Mass.: Xerox College, 1971.

321. Spiegel, John P. THE TRADITION OF VIOLENCE IN OUR SOCIETY. Waltham, Mass.: Brandeis University, 1968.

322. Stanton, Esther. CLIENTS COME LAST: VOLUNTEERS AND WELFARE ORGANIZATIONS. Beverly Hills, Calif.: Sage Publications, 1970.

323. Stearn, Jess. THE SEEKERS. Garden City, N.Y.: Doubleday and Co., 1969.

324. Stebbins, Robert A. COMMITMENT TO DEVIANCE: THE NON-PROFESSIONAL CRIMINAL IN THE COMMUNITY. Westport, Conn.: Greenwood Press, 1971.

325. Stevens, Anita, and Lucy Freeman. I HATE MY PARENTS: THE REAL AND UNREAL REASONS WHY YOUTH IS ANGRY. Chicago, Ill.: Cowles Book Co., 1970.

326. Storr, Anthony. HUMAN AGGRESSION. New York, N. Y.: Atheneum, 1968.

327. Summers, Marvin R. LAW AND ORDER IN A DEMOCRATIC SOCIETY. Columbus, Ohio: C. E. Merrill, 1970.

328. Surface, William. THE POISONED IVY. New York, N.Y.: Coward McCann and Geoghagen, 1968.

329. Suttles, Gerald D. THE SOCIAL ORDER OF THE SLUM. Chicago, Ill.: University of Chicago Press, 1970.

330. Teodori, Massimo. THE NEW LEFT: A DOCUMENTARY HISTORY. Indianapolis, Ind.: Bobbs-Merrill Co., 1969.

331. Thomas, William I. THE UNADJUSTED GIRL WITH CASES AND STANDPOINT FOR BEHAVIOR ANALYSIS. Montclair, N.J.: Patterson Smith, 1969.

332. Tiger, Lionel. MEN IN GROUPS. Westminster, Md.: Random House, 1969.

333. Till, Anthony. WHAT YOU SHOULD KNOW BEFORE YOU BUY A CAR. Los Angeles, Calif.: Sherbourne, 1968.

334. Till, Anthony. WHAT YOU SHOULD KNOW BEFORE YOU HAVE YOUR CAR REPAIRED. Los Angeles, Calif.: Sherbourne, 1970.

335. Time, Incorporated. THE HIPPIES. New York, N.Y.: Grosset and Dunlap, 1967.

336. Toch, Hans. VIOLENT MEN: AN INQUIRY INTO THE PSYCHOLOGY OF VIOLENCE. Chicago, Ill.: Aldine/Atherton, 1969.

337. Travers, Milton. EACH OTHER'S VICTIMS. New York, N.Y.: Charles Scribner's Sons, 1970.

338. Trubowitz, Julius. CHANGING THE RACIAL ATTITUDES OF CHILDREN: THE EFFECTS OF AN ACTIVITY GROUP PROGRAM

IN NEW YORK CITY SCHOOLS. New York, N.Y.: Praeger Publishers, 1969.

339. Ullmann, Leonard. A PSYCHOLOGICAL APPROACH TO ABNOR-MAL BEHAVIOR. Englewood Cliffs, N.J.: Prentice Hall, 1969.

★ 340. U.S. Commission on Civil Rights. FOR ALL PEOPLE, BY ALL PEOPLE, REPORT ON EQUAL OPPORTUNITY IN STATE AND LOCAL GOVERNMENT EMPLOYMENT. Washington, D.C.: U. S. Government Printing Office, 1969.

★ 341. U.S. Commission on Civil Rights. MEXICAN AMERICANS AND THE ADMINISTRATION OF JUSTICE IN THE SOUTHWEST. Washington, D.C.: U.S. Government Printing Office, 1970.

★ 342. U.S. Commission on Civil Rights. RACISM IN AMERICA AND HOW TO COMBAT IT. Washington, D.C.: U.S. Government Printing Office, 1970.

343. U.S. Committee on Government Operations. FEDERAL DATA BANKS, COMPUTERS AND BILL OF RIGHTS, HEARINGS BEFORE SUBCOMMITTEE ON CONSTITUTIONAL RIGHTS, 92nd CONGRESS, 1st SESSION. Washington, D.C.: U.S. Government Printing Office, 1968.

344. U.S. Committee on Internal Security. THE BLACK PANTHER PARTY, ITS ORIGINS AND DEVELOPMENTS. Washington, D.C.: U.S. Government Printing Office, 1970.

345. U.S. Committee on Internal Security. SUBVERSIVE INVOLVE-MENT IN THE ORIGIN, LEADERSHIP, AND ACTIVITIES OF THE NEW MOBILIZATION COMMITTEE TO END THE WAR IN VIET-NAM AND ITS PREDECESSOR ORGANIZATION. Washington, D.C.: U.S. Government Printing Office, 1970.

346. U.S. Committee on Internal Security. THE THEORY AND PRAC-TICE OF COMMUNISM IN 1970. Washington, D.C.: U.S. Government Printing Office, 1970.

347. U.S. House of Representatives Committee on Un-American Activities. THE PRESENT-DAY KU KLUX KLAN MOVEMENT. Washington, D.C.: U.S. Government Printing Office, 1967.

348. U.S. Joint Economic Committee. EMPLOYMENT AND MANPOWER PROBLEMS IN THE CITIES: IMPLICATIONS OF THE REPORT OF THE NATIONAL ADVISORY COMMISSION ON CIVIL DIS-ORDERS; HEARINGS AND REPORT BEFORE 90th CONGRESS, 2nd SESSION (2 parts). Washington, D.C.: U.S. Government Printing Office, 1968.

349. U. S. Labor Department. BREAKTHROUGH FOR DISADVAN-
      TAGED YOUTH. Washington, D.C.: U.S. Government Printing Office,
      1969.

350. U. S. News and World Report. COMMUNISM AND THE NEW LEFT.
      Riverside, N.J.: Macmillan, 1970.

351. U. S. Senate Committee on the Judiciary. COMPUTER PRIVACY,
      HEARINGS BEFORE SUBCOMMITTEE ON ADMINISTRATIVE
      PRACTICE AND PROCEDURES, 90th CONGRESS, 1st SESSION.
      Washington, D.C.: U. S. Government Printing Office, 1967.

352. U. S. Senate Committee on the Judiciary. EXTENT OF SUBVER-
      SION IN THE "NEW LEFT": HEARINGS BEFORE 91st CON-
      GRESS, 2nd SESSION. Washington, D.C.: U. S. Government Printing
      Office, 1970.

353. UNLEARNING PREJUDICE. (Cassette tape, 26 min.) North Holly-
      wood, Calif.: Center for Cassette Studies.

354. Van Waters, Miriam. YOUTH IN CONFLICT. New York, N.Y.: AMS
      Press, 1970.

355. Veysey, Lawrence. LAW AND RESISTANCE: AMERICAN ATTI-
      TUDES TOWARD AUTHORITY. New York, N.Y.: Harper and Row,
      1970.

356. Von Hoffman, Nicholas. WE ARE THE PEOPLE OUR PARENTS
      WARNED US AGAINST. Cleveland, Ohio: Quadrangle Books, 1968.

357. Wagstaff, Thomas. BLACK POWER: THE RADICAL RESPONSE TO
      WHITE AMERICA. Riverside, N.J.: Glencoe Press, 1969.

358. Walsh, Robert E. (ed.). SORRY, NO GOVERNMENT TODAY.
      Boston, Mass.: Beacon Press, 1969.

★ 359. Waskow, Arthur I. RUNNING RIOT: OFFICIAL DISASTERS AND
      CREATIVE DISORDER IN AMERICAN SOCIETY. New York,
      N.Y.: Herder and Herder, 1970.

360. Weaver, Robert C. DILEMMAS OF URBAN AMERICA. New York,
      N.Y.: Atheneum Publishers, 1967.

361. Wein, Bibi. THE RUNAWAY GENERATION. New York, N.Y.:
      Belmont Tower Books, 1972.

362. West, Donald. HOMOSEXUALITY. Chicago, Ill.: Aldine/Atherton,
      1968.

363. Westin, Alan F. PRIVACY AND FREEDOM. New York, N.Y.: Atheneum Publishers, 1967.

★ 364. Williams, W. S. ATTITUDES OF BLACK AND WHITE POLICEMEN TOWARD THE OPPOSITE RACE. Ann Arbor, Mich.: University Microfilm, 1970.

365. Wilson, John Q. CITY POLITICS AND PUBLIC POLICY. New York, N.Y.: John Wiley and Sons, 1968.

366. Wyden, Peter, and Barbara Wyden. GROWING UP STRAIGHT: WHAT EVERY THOUGHTFUL PARENT SHOULD KNOW ABOUT HOMOSEXUALITY. New York, N.Y.: Stein and Day, 1968.

367. Yablonsky, Lewis. THE HIPPIE TRIP. Indianapolis, Ind.: Pegasus, 1968.

368. Young, Whitney M., Jr. BEYOND RACISM: BUILDING AN OPEN SOCIETY. New York, N.Y.: McGraw-Hill, 1969.

CIVIL RIGHTS

See also **Behavioral and Social Science**   **Planning and Evaluation**
Crime Deterrence and Prevention   **Riot Control and Urban**
Juvenile Delinquency   **Disorders**
Judicial Process   **Student Disorders**
Laws and Statutes

369. Abernathy, M. Glenn. CIVIL LIBERTIES UNDER THE CONSTITUTION. New York, N.Y.: Dodd, Mead & Co., 1968.

★ 370. Asch, Sidney. POLICE AUTHORITY AND THE RIGHTS OF THE INDIVIDUAL. New York, N.Y.: Arco Publishing Co., 1968.

371. Association of the Bar of the City of New York. Special Committee on Radio, Television and the Administration of Justice. FREEDOM OF THE PRESS AND FAIR TRIAL: FINAL REPORT WITH RECOMMENDATIONS. New York, N.Y.: Columbia University Press, 1967.

★ 372. Blaustein, Albert P., and Robert Zangrando. CIVIL RIGHTS AND THE AMERICAN NEGRO: A DOCUMENTARY HISTORY. New York, N.Y.: Washington Square Press, 1968.

373. Carey, John. UNPROTECTION OF CIVIL AND POLITICAL RIGHTS. Syracuse, N.Y.: Syracuse University Press, 1970.

374.   Conant, Ralph. PROSPECTS FOR REVOLUTION: A STUDY OF RIOTS, CIVIL DISOBEDIENCE AND INSURRECTION IN CONTEMPORARY AMERICA. New York, N.Y.: Harper and Row, 1971.

375.   Dorsen, Norman (ed.). RIGHTS OF AMERICANS: WHAT THEY ARE—WHAT THEY SHOULD BE. New York, N.Y.: Pantheon Books, 1971.

376.   Douglas, William O. ANATOMY OF LIBERTY. New York, N.Y.: Simon and Schuster, 1967.

377.   Eidelberg, Paul. THE PHILOSOPHY OF THE AMERICAN CONSTITUTION: A REINTERPRETATION OF THE INTENTIONS OF THE FOUNDING FATHERS. Riverside, N.J.: Free Press, 1968.

378.   Emerson, Thomas I. POLITICAL AND CIVIL RIGHTS IN THE UNITED STATES (2 vols.). Waltham, Mass.: Little, Brown and Co., 1967.

379.   Fisher, Charles. MINORITIES, CIVIL RIGHTS AND PROTEST. Ralston Park, Belmont, Calif.: Dickenson Publishing Co., 1970.

380.   Fortas, Abe. CONCERNING DISSENT AND CIVIL DISOBEDIENCE. New York, N.Y.: New American Library, 1968.

381.   Fraenkel, Osmond. RIGHTS WE HAVE. New York, N.Y.: Thomas Y. Crowell, 1971.

382.   FREE PRESS AND FAIR TRIAL. (Cassette tape, 28 min.) North Hollywood, Calif.: Center for Cassette Studies.

383.   Friedman, Leon. THE CIVIL RIGHTS READER. New York, N.Y.: Walker and Co., 1967.

384.   Gillers, Stephen. GETTING JUSTICE: THE RIGHTS OF PEOPLE. New York, N.Y.: Basic Books, 1971.

385.   Hass, Ernest. HUMAN RIGHTS AND INTERNATIONAL ACTION: THE CASE OF FREEDOM OF ASSOCIATION. Stanford, Calif.: Stanford University Press, 1970.

386.   Konvitz, Milton (ed.). BILL OF RIGHTS READER: LEADING CONSTITUTIONAL CASES. Ithaca, N.Y.: Cornell University Press, 1968.

★ 387.   McCafferty, James (ed.). CAPITAL PUNISHMENT. Chicago, Ill.: Aldine/Atherton, 1972.

388. McCord, John. WITH ALL DELIBERATE SPEED: CIVIL RIGHTS THEORY AND REALITY. Urbana, Ill.: University of Illinois Press, 1969.

389. Meldén, A. I. HUMAN RIGHTS. Belmont, Calif.: Wadsworth Publishing Co., 1970.

390. Muse, Benjamin. AMERICAN NEGRO REVOLUTION FROM NON-VIOLENCE TO BLACK POWER. Bloomington, Ind.: Indiana University Press, 1968.

391. Newman, Edwin. CIVIL LIBERTY AND CIVIL RIGHTS. Dobbs Ferry, N.Y.: Oceana Publications, 1970.

392. Ratcliffe, Robert, and others. VITAL ISSUES OF THE CONSTITUTION. Boston, Mass.: Houghton-Mifflin, 1971.

393. THE RIGHT OF CONFRONTATION. (Cassette tape, 27 min.) North Hollywood, Calif.: Center for Cassette Studies.

394. THE RIGHT TO LEGAL COUNSEL. (16mm color, 14 min.) Santa Monica, Calif.: BFA Educational Media.

395. THE RIGHT TO REMAIN SILENT. (Cassette tape, 27 min.) North Hollywood, Calif.: Center for Cassette Studies.

396. Rodgers, Harrell R., and Charles S. Bullock. LAW AND SOCIAL CHANGE: CIVIL RIGHTS AND THEIR CONSEQUENCES. New York, N.Y.: McGraw-Hill, 1972.

397. Rustin, Bayard. DOWN THE LINE. New York, N.Y.: Quadrangle Books, 1971.

398. Silverman, Sondra. BLACK REVOLT AND DEMOCRATIC POLITICS. Indianapolis, Ind.: D. C. Heath Co., 1970.

399. Van Dyke, Vernon. HUMAN RIGHTS, THE UNITED STATES AND WORLD COMMUNITY. New York, N.Y.: Oxford University Press, 1970.

400. Zarr, Melvyn. THE BILL OF RIGHTS AND THE POLICE. Dobbs Ferry, N.Y.: Oceana Publishing, 1970.

See also   Behavioral and Social Science   Juvenile Delinquency
Civil Rights   Laws and Statutes
Crime Deterrence and Prevention Organized Crime
Criminal Investigation   Student Disorders
Criminology   Victimless Crime
Judicial Process

401. Alexander, Alfred, and Val Moolman. STEALING. New York, N.Y.: Cornerstone Library, 1968.

402. American Humane Association. SEXUAL ABUSE OF CHILDREN: IMPLICATIONS FOR CASE-WORK. Denver, Colo.: American Humane Association, 1967.

403. Amir, Menachem. PATTERNS IN FORCIBLE RAPE. Chicago, Ill.: University of Chicago Press, 1971.

404. Barnes, Robert, and Ronald Sarro. ARE YOU SAFE FROM BURGLARS. Garden City, N.Y.: Doubleday and Co., 1971.

405. Brindy, James. SHOPLIFTING: MANUAL FOR STORE DETEC-TIVES. Matteson, Ill.: Cavalier Press, 1970.

406. CHILD MOLESTER. (16mm color, 20 min.) Mansfield, Ohio: High-way Safety Foundation.

407. THE CHILD MOLESTER. (Sound filmstrip, color.) Gaithersburg, Md.: International Association of Chiefs of Police.

408. Ducovny, Amram. THE BILLION DOLLAR SWINDLE: FRAUDS AGAINST THE ELDERLY. New York, N.Y.: Fleet Press, 1969.

409. Elmer, Elizabeth. CHILDREN IN JEOPARDY: A STUDY OF ABUSED MINORS AND THEIR FAMILIES. Pittsburgh, Pa.: University of Pittsburgh Press, 1967.

410. Fitch, Richard D., and Edward A. Porter. ACCIDENTAL OR INCENDIARY. Springfield, Ill.: Charles C. Thomas, 1968.

411. Fontana, Vincent J. THE MALTREATED CHILD: THE MAL-TREATMENT SYNDROME IN CHILDREN. Springfield, Ill.: Charles C. Thomas, 1971.

412. Gaddis, Thomas E., and James O. Long. KILLER: A JOURNAL OF MURDER. Riverside, N.J.: Macmillan Co., 1970.

★ 413. Geis, Gilbert. WHITE-COLLAR CRIMINAL: THE OFFENDER IN BUSINESS AND THE PROFESSIONS. Chicago, Ill.: Aldine/Atherton, 1968.

414. Gil, David. VIOLENCE AGAINST CHILDREN: PHYSICAL CHILD ABUSE IN THE U.S. Cambridge, Mass.: Harvard University Press, 1970.

415. Glaser, Daniel. ADULT CRIME AND SOCIAL POLICY. Englewood Cliffs, N.J.: Prentice Hall, 1972.

416. Graham, Fred P. THE SELF-INFLICTED WOUND. Riverside, N.J.: Macmillan Co., 1970.

417. Green, Timothy. THE SMUGGLERS. New York, N.Y.: Walker and Co., 1969.

418. Heaps, Willard A. ASSASSINATION: A SPECIAL KIND OF MUR-DER. New York, N.Y.: Hawthorn Books, 1969.

★ 419. Helfer, Ray, and C. Henry Kemp. THE BATTERED CHILD. Chicago, Ill.: University of Chicago Press, 1968.

420. HOMICIDE. (Sound filmstrip, color.) Gaithersburg, Md.: International Association of Chiefs of Police.

421. Hubbard, David. THE SKYJACKER. Riverside, N.J.: Macmillan and 1971.

422. Irwin, John. THE FELON. Englewood Cliffs, N.J.: Prentice Hall, 1970.

★ 423. Iskrant, Albert P., and Paul V. Juliet. ACCIDENTS AND HOMICIDE. Cambridge, Mass.: Harvard University Press, 1968.

424. Leitch, David. THE DISCRIMINATING THIEF. New York, N.Y.: Holt, Rinehart and Winston, 1969.

425. Levy, Sheldon, and others. ASSASSINATION AND POLITICAL VIOLENCE. Washington, D.C.: U. S. Government Printing Office, 1969.

426. MacDonald, J. M. HOMICIDAL THREATS. Springfield, Ill.: Charles C. Thomas, 1968.

427. MacDonald, John. RAPE OFFENDERS AND THEIR VICTIMS. Springfield, Ill.: Charles C. Thomas, 1971.

428. Madison, Arnold. VANDALISM: THE NOT-SO-SENSELESS CRIME. New York, N.Y.:Seabury Press, 1970.

429. Margolius, Sidney. THE INNOCENT CONSUMER VS THE EXPLOIT-ERS. New York, N.Y.: Trident Press, 1967.

430. Parker, Tony. THE HIDDEN WORLD OF SEX OFFENDERS. Indianapolis, Ind.: Bobbs-Merrill, 1969.

431. Polsky, Ned. HUSTLERS, BEATS, AND OTHERS. Chicago, Ill.: Aldine/Atherton, 1967.

432. PROWLER. (Sound filmstrip, color.) Gaithersburg, Md.: International Association of Chiefs of Police.

433. Rappeport, Jonas R. THE CLINICAL EVALUATION OF THE DANGEROUSNESS OF THE MENTALLY ILL. Springfield, Ill.: Charles C. Thomas, 1967.

434. ROBBERY. (Sound filmstrip, color.) Gaithersburg, Md.: International Association of Chiefs of Police.

435. Smigel, Erwin, and Hugh Ross. CRIMES AGAINST BUREAUCRACY. Cincinnati, Ohio: Van Nostrand Reinhold Co., 1970.

436. Springer, John L. CONSUMER SWINDLERS AND HOW TO AVOID THEM. Chicago, Ill.: Henry Regnery Co., 1970.

437. U. S. Center for Studies in Crime and Delinquency. National Institute of Mental Health. THE MENTALLY RETARDED OFFENDER. Washington, D.C.: U. S. Government Printing Office, 1971.

438. U. S. Committee on Un-American Activities. CONDUCT OF ESPIONAGE WITHIN THE UNITED STATES BY AGENTS OF FOREIGN COMMUNIST GOVERNMENTS: HEARINGS BEFORE... 90th CONGRESS, 1st SESSION. Washington, D.C.: U. S. Government Printing Office, 1971.

439. U. S. Law Enforcement Assistance Administration. THE CRIME OF ROBBERY IN THE UNITED STATES. Washington, D.C.: U. S. Government Printing Office, 1971.

440. U. S. Law Enforcement Assistance Administration. THE NATURE, IMPACT AND PROSECUTION OF WHITE COLLAR CRIME. Washington, D.C.: U. S. Government Printing Office, 1970.

441. U. S. National Commission on Prevention of Violence. ASSASSINA-TION AND POLITICAL VIOLENCE. Washington, D.C.: U. S. Government Printing Office, 1969.

442. U. S. National Commission on Prevention of Violence. CRIMES OF VIOLENCE. Washington, D.C.: U. S. Government Printing Office, 1969.

443. U. S. Post Office Department. MAIL FRAUD LAW—PROTECTING CONSUMERS, INVESTORS, BUSINESSMEN, MEDICAL PATIENTS, STUDENTS. Washington, D.C.: U. S. Government Printing Office, 1969.

444. U. S. President's Task Force on Prisoner Rehabilitation. THE CRIMINAL OFFENDER—WHAT SHOULD BE DONE? Washington, D.C.: U. S. Government Printing Office, 1970.

445. Wise, David, and Thomas B. Ross. THE ESPIONAGE ESTABLISHMENT. Westminster, Md.: Random House, 1967.

COMMUNICATIONS:
DATA/VISUAL/VOICE/EQUIPMENT

See also **Information: Systems/Software**   **Police Traffic Function**
Police Equipment   **Security Systems**
Police Patrol Function   **Training**

★ 446. Burton, Alan. POLICE TELECOMMUNICATIONS. Springfield, Ill.: Charles C. Thomas, 1972.

447. Carlson, A. Bruce. COMMUNICATION SYSTEMS: AN INTRODUCTION TO SIGNALS AND NOISE IN ELECTRICAL COMMUNICATION. New York, N.Y.: McGraw-Hill, 1968.

448. Davenport, William. MODERN DATA COMMUNICATIONS: CONCEPTS, LANGUAGE AND MEDIA. New York, N.Y.: Hayden Book Co., 1971.

449. Drabek, Thomas. LABORATORY SIMULATION OF A POLICE COMMUNICATIONS SYSTEM UNDER STRESS. Columbus, Ohio: Ohio State University, 1969.

★ 450. Leonard, V. A. POLICE COMMUNICATIONS SYSTEM. Springfield, Ill.: Charles C. Thomas, 1970.

451. Mambent, W. A. PRESENTING TECHNICAL IDEAS: A GUIDE TO AUDIENCE COMMUNICATION. New York, N.Y.: John Wiley and Sons, 1968.

452. Martin, James. TELECOMMUNICATIONS AND THE COMPUTER. Englewood Cliffs, N.J.: Prentice Hall, 1969.

453. Martin, James. TELEPROCESSING NETWORK ORGANIZATION. Englewood Cliffs, N.J.: Prentice Hall, 1970.

454. Mathison, Stuart, and Philip Walker. COMPUTERS AND TELE-COMMUNICATIONS: ISSUES IN PUBLIC POLICY. Englewood Cliffs, N.J.: Prentice Hall, 1970.

455. Meadow, C. T. MAN-MACHINE COMMUNICATION. New York, N.Y.: John Wiley and Sons, 1970.

456. Michigan Department of State Police. VOICE IDENTIFICATION RESEARCH. Washington, D.C.: U. S. Government Printing Office, 1972.

457. Murgio, Matthew. COMMUNICATIONS GRAPHICS. Cincinnati, Ohio: Van Nostrand Reinhold Co., 1969.

458. Oringel, Robert. AUDIO CONTROL HANDBOOK: FOR RADIO AND TELEVISION BROADCASTING. New York, N.Y.: Hastings House, 1972.

459. Passman, Sidney. SCIENTIFIC AND TECHNOLOGICAL COMMUN-ICATION. Elmsford, N.Y.: Pergamon Press, 1969.

460. Thayer, Lee. COMMUNICATION AND COMMUNICATION SYS-TEMS: IN ORGANIZATION, MANAGEMENT AND INTERPER-SONAL RELATIONS. Homewood, Ill.: Richard D. Irwin, 1968.

461. U. S. Law Enforcement Assistance Administration. THE APCO PROJECT—A NATIONAL TRAINING MANUAL AND PROCE-DURAL GUIDE FOR POLICE AND PUBLIC SAFETY RADIO COMMUNICATIONS PERSONNEL. Washington, D.C.: U. S. Government Printing Office, 1968.

★ 462. U. S. Law Enforcement Assistance Administration. POLICE TELE-COMMUNICATION SYSTEMS. Washington, D.C.: U. S. Government Printing Office, 1971.

463. Vardaman, George T. EFFECTIVE COMMUNICATION OF IDEAS. Cincinnati, Ohio: Van Nostrand Reinhold Co., 1970.

COMMUNITY BASED CORRECTIONS:
ADULT/JUVENILE

See also Community Relations
Correctional Institutions:
    Adult/Juvenile
Jails
Judicial Process

Juvenile Court
Laws and Statutes
Probation and Parole:
    Adult/Juvenile

★ 464. Keller, Oliver J. HALFWAY HOUSES: COMMUNITY-CENTERED CORRECTION AND TREATMENT. Indianapolis, Ind.: D. C. Heath and Co., 1970.

465. President's Task Force on Prisoner Rehabilitation. CRIMINAL OFFENDER: WHAT SHOULD BE DONE. Washington, D.C.: U. S. Government Printing Office, 1970.

★ 466. Saleebey, George. THE NON-PRISON: A NEW APPROACH TO TREATING YOUTHFUL OFFENDERS. New Rochelle, N.Y.: Bruce, 1970.

COMMUNITY: INVOLVEMENT/RELATIONS

See also Behavioral and Social Science
Domestic Relations
Police Patrol Functions
Police Traffic Functions

Riot Control and Urban
    Disorders
Student Disorders
Training

★ 467. Adams, Thomas F. LAW ENFORCEMENT: AN INTRODUCTION TO THE POLICE ROLE IN THE COMMUNITY. Englewood Cliffs, N.J.: Prentice Hall, 1968.

468. Bayley, David, and H. Mendelsohn. MINORITIES AND THE POLICE: CONFRONTATION IN AMERICA. Riverside, N.J.: Free Press, 1969.

★ 469. Black, Algernon. THE PEOPLE AND THE POLICE. New York, N.Y.: McGraw-Hill, 1968.

★ 470. Bouma, Donald H. KIDS AND COPS: A STUDY IN MUTUAL HOSTILITY. Grand Rapids, Mich.: William B. Eerdmans Publishing Co., 1969.

471. Brandstatter, A. F., and Louis A. Radelet. POLICE & COMMUNITY RELATIONS: A SOURCEBOOK. Riverside, N.J.: Glencoe Press, 1968.

472. Chamber of Commerce of the U. S. MARSHALING CITIZEN POWER AGAINST CRIME. Washington, D.C.: Chamber of Commerce of the U. S., 1970.

★ 473. Coffey, Alan. POLICE-COMMUNITY RELATIONS. Englewood Cliffs, N.J.: Prentice Hall, 1971.

★ 474. Earle, Howard H. POLICE-COMMUNITY RELATIONS: CRISIS IN OUR TIME. Springfield, Ill.: Charles C. Thomas, 1970.

475. Edwards, George. THE POLICE ON THE URBAN FRONTIER: A GUIDE TO COMMUNITY UNDERSTANDING. New York, N.Y.: American Jewish Community, 1968.

476. Hahn, Harlan (ed.). POLICE IN URBAN SOCIETY. Beverly Hills, Calif.: Sage Publications, 1971.

477. Hallman, Howard. NEIGHBORHOOD CONTROL OF PUBLIC PRO-GRAMS. New York, N.Y.: Praeger Publishers, 1970.

478. Hewitt, William H. POLICE AND COMMUNITY RELATIONS: AN ANTHOLOGY AND BIBLIOGRAPHY. Mineola, N.Y.: Foundation Press, 1970.

479. Holcomb, Richard L. THE POLICE AND THE PUBLIC. Springfield, Ill.: Charles C. Thomas, 1971.

480. IMPROVING THE OFFICER-CITIZEN CONTACT. (Sound film-strip, color.) Gaithersburg, Md.: International Association of Chiefs of Police.

481. Knopf, Terry. YOUTH PATROLS: AN EXPERIMENT IN COMMUN-ITY PARTICIPATION. Waltham, Mass.: Brandeis University, 1969.

482. Lambert, John R. CRIME, POLICE, AND RACE RELATIONS: A STUDY IN BIRMINGHAM. New York, N.Y.: Oxford University Press, 1970.

483. MAN IN THE MIDDLE. (16mm b&w, 22 min.) New York, N.Y.: Anti-Defamation League of B'nai B'rith.

484. Mendelsohn, Harold, and D. H. Bayley. MINORITIES AND THE POLICE. New York, N.Y.: Free Press, 1971.

★ 485. Momboisse, Raymond M. COMMUNITY RELATIONS AND RIOT PREVENTION. Springfield, Ill.: Charles C. Thomas, 1967.

486. THE POSITIVE IMAGE. (16mm color, 20 min.) Washington, D.C.: Federal Bureau of Investigation.

487. Poston, Richard W. THE GANG AND THE ESTABLISHMENT. New York, N.Y.: Harper and Row, 1971.

488. Rosenbloom, Richard, and Robin Morris. SOCIAL INNOVATION IN THE CITY: NEW ENTERPRISES FOR COMMUNITY DEVELOP-MENT. Cambridge, Mass.: Harvard University Press, 1969.

489. SAY HELLO TO A COP TODAY. (Cassette tape, 44 min.) North Hollywood, Calif.: Center for Cassette Studies.

★ 490. Strecher, Victor. THE ENVIRONMENT OF LAW ENFORCEMENT: A COMMUNITY RELATIONS GUIDE. Englewood Cliffs, N.J.: Prentice Hall, 1971.

491. Taber, Merlin, and others. HANDBOOK FOR COMMUNITY PRO-FESSIONALS: AN APPROACH FOR PLANNING AND ACTION. Springfield, Ill.: Charles C. Thomas, 1972.

492. TAKE ANOTHER LOOK. (16mm color, 20 min.) Burbank, Calif.: Wickham Films.

493. Wallach, I. A. POLICE FUNCTIONS IN A NEGRO COMMUNITY (2 vols.) Springfield, Va.: National Technical Information Service, 1970.

494. Watson, Nelson A. IMPROVING THE OFFICER-CITIZEN CON-TACT. Gaithersburg, Md.: International Association of Chiefs of Police, 1968.

495. Weinberg, I. C. VOLUNTEERS HELP YOUTH. Washington, D.C.: U. S. Government Printing Office, 1971.

496. Weissman, Harold (ed.). COMMUNITY DEVELOPMENT IN THE MOBILIZATION OF YOUTH EXPERIENCE. New York, N.Y.: Association Press, 1969.

CORRECTIONAL INSTITUTIONS:
ADULT/JUVENILE

See also **Behavioral and Social Science**   **Judicial Process**
Community Based Corrections: **Laws and Statutes**
    Adult/Juvenile   **Probation and Parole:**
Jails   **Adult/Juvenile**

497. Baird, Russell N. THE PENAL PRESS. Evanston, Ill.: Northwestern University Press, 1967.

498. Brodsky, Stanley L. THE MILITARY PRISON: THEORY, RESEARCH, AND PRACTICE. Carbondale, Ill.: South Illinois University Press, 1970.

499. CAGES ARE FOR ANIMALS. (Cassette tape, 54 min.) North Hollywood, Calif.: Center for Cassette Studies.

★ 500. CHILDREN IN CAGES. (Cassette tape, 49 min.) North Hollywood, Calif.: Center for Cassette Studies.

501. Cohen, Fred. THE LEGAL CHALLENGE TO CORRECTIONS: IMPLICATIONS FOR MANPOWER AND TRAINING. Washington, D.C.: U. S. Government Printing Office, 1969.

502. Dix, Dorothea Lynde. REMARKS ON PRISONS AND PRISON DISCIPLINE IN THE U.S. Montclair, N.J.: J. P. Smith, 1967.

503. Downey, J. J. STATE RESPONSIBILITY FOR JUVENILE DETENTION CARE. Washington, D.C.: U. S. Government Printing Office, 1970.

504. Eyman, Joy G. PRISONS FOR WOMEN: A PRACTICAL GUIDE TO ADMINISTRATION PROBLEMS. Springfield, Ill.: Charles C. Thomas, 1971.

505. Fenton, Norman. THE CORRECTIONAL COMMUNITY: AN INTRODUCTION AND GUIDE. Berkeley, Calif.: University of California Press, 1967.

506. Giallombardo, Rose. SOCIETY OF WOMEN: A STUDY OF A WOMAN'S PRISON. New York, N.Y.: John Wiley and Sons, 1970.

507. Hazelrigg, Lawrence E. (ed.). PRISON WITHIN SOCIETY: A READER IN PENOLOGY. Garden City, N.Y.: Doubleday and Co., 1968.

508. Heffernan, C. G. MAKING IT IN PRISON: THE SQUARE, THE COOL, AND THE LIFE. New York, N.Y.: Wiley-Interscience, 1972.

509. Hopper, Columbus B. SEX IN PRISON: THE MISSISSIPPI EXPERIMENT WITH CONJUGAL VISITING. Baton Rouge, La.: Louisiana State University Press, 1969.

★ 510. Ives, George. A HISTORY OF PENAL METHODS: CRIMINALS, WITCHES, LUNATICS. Montclair, N.J.: Paterson-Smith, 1970.

★ 511. Johnston, Norman (ed.). THE SOCIOLOGY OF PUNISHMENT AND CORRECTION. New York, N.Y.: John Wiley and Sons, 1970.

512. Joint Commission on Corrections Manpower and Training. A CLIMATE FOR CHANGE. Washington, D.C.: American Correctional Association, 1968.

513. Joint Commission on Corrections Manpower and Training. THE LEGAL CHALLENGE TO CORRECTIONS: IMPLICATIONS FOR MANPOWER AND TRAINING. Washington, D.C.: American Correctional Association, 1969.

514. Joint Committee on Corrections Manpower and Training. UNIVERSITY AND CORRECTIONS POTENTIAL FOR COLLABORATIVE RELATIONSHIPS. Washington, D.C.: American Correctional Association, 1969.

515. Kandle, George C., and Henry H. Gassler. MINISTERING TO PRISONERS AND THEIR FAMILIES. Philadelphia, Pa.: Fortress Press, 1969.

516. Kassebaum, Gene. PRISON TREATMENT AND PAROLE SURVIVAL: AN EMPIRICAL ASSESSMENT. New York, N.Y.: John Wiley and Sons, 1971.

517. MacNamara, Donald E. J., and Edward Sagarin (eds.). PERSPECTIVES ON CORRECTION. New York, N.Y.: Thomas Y. Crowell Co., 1971.

518. Manocchio, Anthony J. THE TIME GAME: TWO VIEWS OF A PRISON. Beverly Hills, Calif.: Sage Publications, 1970.

★ 519. Miller, Frank. THE CORRECTIONAL PROCESS. Mineola, N.Y.: Foundation Press, 1971.

520. Minton, Robert J. (ed.). INSIDE: PRISON AMERICAN STYLE. Westminster, Md.: Random House, 1972.

521. New York (State). Committee on Mental Health Services Inside and Outside the Family Court in the City of New York. JUVENILE JUSTICE CONFOUNDED: PRETENSIONS AND REALITIES OF TREATMENT SERVICES. New York, N.Y.: National Council on Crime and Delinquency, 1972.

522. Parker, Tony. THE FRYING PAN: A PRISON AND ITS PRISONERS. New York, N.Y.: Basic Books, 1970.

★ 523. Perlman, Harvey S., and Thomas B. Allington (eds.). THE TASKS OF PENOLOGY: A SYMPOSIUM ON PRISONS AND CORRECTIONAL LAW. Lincoln, Neb.: University of Nebraska Press, 1969.

524. Roberts, Albert. SOURCEBOOK ON PRISON EDUCATION: PAST, PRESENT, AND FUTURE. Springfield, Ill.: Charles C. Thomas, 1971.

★ 525. Rubin, Sol. CRIME AND JUVENILE DELINQUENCY: A RATIONAL APPROACH TO PENAL PROBLEMS. Dobbs Ferry, N.Y.: Oceana Publications, 1970.

526. Studt, Elliot. C-UNIT: SEARCH FOR COMMUNITY IN PRISON. New York, N.Y.: Russell Sage Foundation, 1968.

527. U. S. Bureau of Prisons. PRISONER MANAGEMENT AND CONTROL. Washington, D.C.: U. S. Bureau of Prisons, 1969.

528. U. S. Center for Studies in Crime and Delinquency. National Institute of Mental Health. COMMUNITY BASED CORRECTIONAL PROGRAMS, MODELS AND PRACTICES. Washington, D.C.: U. S. Government Printing Office, 1971.

★ 529. U. S. Law Enforcement Assistance Administration. NEW ENVIRONMENTS FOR THE INCARCERATED. Washington, D.C.: U. S. Department of Justice, 1972.

530. U. S. Law Enforcement Assistance Administration. OUTSIDE LOOKING IN: A SERIES OF MONOGRAPHS ASSESSING THE EFFECTIVENESS OF CORRECTIONS. Washington, D.C.: U. S. Law Enforcement Assistance Administration, 1971.

531. U. S. Bureau of Prisons. THE RESIDENTIAL CENTER: CORRECTIONS IN THE COMMUNITY. Washington, D.C.: U. S. Bureau of Prisons, 1971.

532. U. S. Office of Juvenile Delinquency and Youth Development. THE CRISIS OF QUALIFIED MANPOWER FOR CRIMINAL JUSTICE, AN ANALYTIC ASSESSMENT WITH GUIDELINES FOR NEW POLICY: CORRECTIONAL INSTITUTIONS. Washington, D.C.: U. S. Government Printing Office, 1969.

533. Vedder, Clyde, and Barbara Kay. PENOLOGY: A REALISTIC APPROACH. Springfield, Ill.: Charles C. Thomas, 1969.

534. Wilkins, Leslie T. EVALUATION OF PENAL MEASURES. Westminster, Md.: Random House, 1969.

COURT:
MANAGEMENT AND OPERATION/STRUCTURE

See also **Judicial Process**   **Prosecution**
Laws and Statutes

535. Council of State Governments. STATE COURT SYSTEMS: A
      STATISTICAL SUMMARY. Lexington, Ky.: Council of State
      Governments, 1970.

536. Jennings, J. B. QUANTITATIVE MODELS OF CRIMINAL COURTS.
      Santa Monica, Calif.: Rand Corporation, 1971.

537. Saari, David. MODERN COURT MANAGEMENT—TRENDS IN THE
      ROLE OF THE COURT EXECUTIVE. Washington, D.C.: U. S.
      Government Printing Office, 1970.

538. Sheldon, Charles. THE SUPREME COURT: POLITICIANS IN
      ROBES. Riverside, N.J.: Glencoe Press, 1970.

539. Sigler, Jay A. THE COURTS AND PUBLIC POLICY. Homewood,
      Ill.: Dorsey Press, 1970.

CRIME DETERRENCE AND PREVENTION

See also **Behavioral and Social Science   Planning and Evaluation**
Criminal Investigation   Police Equipment
Criminalistics   Police Patrol Function
Criminology   Police Traffic Function
Education   Security Systems
Information: Systems/Software   Support Services
Judicial Process   Training
Laws and Statutes

540. American Friends Service Commission. STRUGGLE FOR JUSTICE:
      A REPORT ON CRIME AND PUNISHMENT IN AMERICA. New
      York, N.Y.: Hill and Wang, 1971.

541. BURGLARY PREVENTION. (Sound filmstrip, color.) Gaithersburg,
      Md.: International Association of Chiefs of Police.

542. California State College. AERIAL SURVEILLANCE METHODS OF
      CRIME PREVENTION—EVALUATION. Los Angeles, Calif.: California
      State College, 1968.

543. Committee for Economic Development. REDUCING CRIME AND ASSURING JUSTICE. New York, N.Y.: Committee for Economic Development, 1972.

544. CRIME AND ITS PREVENTION. (Sound filmstrip, color.) Gaithersburg, Md.: International Association of Chiefs of Police.

545. Elliott, James. CRIME CONTROL TEAM: AN EXPERIMENT IN MUNICIPAL POLICE DEPARTMENT MANAGEMENT AND OPERATIONS. Springfield, Ill.: Charles C. Thomas, 1971.

546. Empey, Lamar. ALTERNATIVES TO INCARCERATION. Washington, D.C.: U. S. Office of Juvenile Delinquency and Youth Development, 1967.

547. Hair, Robert, and Sara Baker. HOW TO PROTECT YOURSELF TODAY. New York, N.Y.: Pocket Books, 1971.

548. Institute for Defense Analyses. NATIONAL PROGRAM OF RESEARCH, DEVELOPMENT, TEST AND EVALUATION ON LAW ENFORCEMENT AND CRIMINAL JUSTICE. Washington, D.C.: U. S. Government Printing Office, 1968.

★ 549. Jeffery, C. Ray. CRIME PREVENTION THROUGH ENVIRONMENTAL DESIGN. Beverly Hills, Calif.: Sage Publications, 1971.

550. Johnston, Norman. THE SOCIOLOGY OF PUNISHMENT AND CORRECTION. New York, N.Y.: John Wiley and Sons, 1970.

551. Kaufmann, Ulrich. HOW TO AVOID BURGLARY, HOUSE-BREAKING AND OTHER CRIMES. New York, N.Y.: Crown Publishers, 1967.

552. Kirkpatrick, R., and R. C. Stevens. COMPREHENSIVE RESEARCH PROGRAM IN CRIME PREVENTION. Springfield, Va.: National Technical Information Service, 1969.

★ 553. Knopf, Terry Ann. YOUTH PATROLS: AN EXPERIMENT IN COMMUNITY PARTICIPATION. Waltham, Mass.: Brandeis University, 1969.

554. Lewin, Stephen. CRIME AND ITS PREVENTION. New York, N.Y.: H. W. Wilson Co., 1968.

555. Madden, Edward H. PHILOSOPHICAL PERSPECTIVES ON PUNISHMENT. Springfield, Ill.: Charles C. Thomas, 1968.

556. Menninger, Karl A. THE CRIME OF PUNISHMENT. New York, N.Y.: Viking Press, 1968.

557. Middendorff, Wolf. THE EFFECTIVENESS OF PUNISHMENT. South Hackensack, N.J.: Fred B. Rothman and Co., 1968.

558. Moolman, Val. PRACTICAL WAYS TO PREVENT BURGLARY AND ILLEGAL ENTRY. New York, N.Y.: Cornerstone Library, 1970.

559. Morris, Norval, and Gordon Hawkins. THE HONEST POLITICIAN'S GUIDE TO CRIME CONTROL. Chicago, Ill.: University of Chicago Press, 1970.

560. Mundis, Jerrold J. THE GUARD DOGS. New York, N.Y.: David McKay, 1970.

★ 561. Pursuit, Dan, and others. POLICE PROGRAMS FOR PREVENTING CRIME AND DELINQUENCY. Springfield, Ill.: Charles C. Thomas, 1972.

562. Rusche, George, and Otto Kirchheimer. PUNISHMENT AND SOCIAL STRUCTURE. New York, N.Y.: Russell and Russell, 1968.

563. Smith, R. Dean, and Richard W. Kobetz. GUIDELINES FOR CIVIL DISORDER AND MOBILIZATION PLANNING: PREPARED FOR THE PRESIDENT'S ADVISORY COMMISSION ON CIVIL DISORDERS. Gaithersburg, Md.: International Association of Chiefs of Police, 1968.

564. U.S. Center for Studies in Crime and Delinquency. National Institute of Mental Health. PERSPECTIVES ON DETERRENCE. Washington, D.C.: U.S. Government Printing Office, 1971.

565. U.S. Committee on the Judiciary. PREVENTIVE DETENTION. Washington, D.C.: U.S. Government Printing Office, 1970.

566. U.S. Department of Justice. THE WAVE OF CRIME WILL NOT BE THE WAVE OF THE FUTURE: PRESIDENT NIXON'S PROPOSAL FOR LAW ENFORCEMENT REVENUE SHARING. Washington, D.C.: U.S. Government Printing Office, 1971.

★ 567. U.S. Law Enforcement Assistance Administration. PLANNING GUIDELINES AND PROGRAMS TO REDUCE CRIME. Washington, D.C.: U.S. Department of Justice, 1972.

568. U.S. Law Enforcement Assistance Administration. SAFE STREETS: THE LEAA PROGRAM AT WORK. Washington, D.C.: U.S. Department of Justice, 1971.

569. U.S. National Commission on Prevention of Violence. MASS MEDIA AND VIOLENCE. Washington, D.C.: U.S. Government Printing Office, 1969.

570. U.S. Youth Development and Delinquency Prevention Administration. DIVERTING YOUTH FROM THE CORRECTIONAL SYSTEM. Washington, D.C.: U.S. Youth Development and Delinquency Prevention Administration, 1971.

571. U.S. Youth Development and Delinquency Prevention Administration. LAW AS AN AGENT OF DELINQUENCY PREVENTION. Washington, D.C.: U.S. Government Printing Office, 1971.

572. White, Bertha R. CRIME AND PENALTIES. Dobbs Ferry, N.Y.: Oceana Publishing, 1970.

CRIMINAL INVESTIGATION

See also **Behavioral and Social Science**   **Information Systems**
Communications   **Planning and Evaluation**
Crime Deterrence and Prevention   **Police Equipment**
Criminalistics   **Police Patrol Function**
Criminology   **Training**

573. Arons, H. HYPNOSIS IN CRIMINAL INVESTIGATION. Springfield, Ill.: Charles C. Thomas, 1967.

574. Arther, Richard O. THE SCIENTIFIC INVESTIGATOR. Springfield, Ill.: Charles C. Thomas, 1970.

575. Asch, Sidney. POLICE AUTHORITY AND THE RIGHTS OF THE INDIVIDUAL. New York, N.Y.: Arco Books, 1968.

576. ASPECTS OF SCIENTIFIC INVESTIGATION. (Sound filmstrip, color.) Gaithersburg, Md.: International Association of Chiefs of Police.

577. Aubrey, Arthur, and Rudolph Caputo. CRIMINAL INTERROGATION. Springfield, Ill.: Charles C. Thomas, 1972.

578. Chaffee, Zechariah, and others. THE THIRD DEGREE. New York, N.Y.: Arno Press, 1969.

579. Chilmidos, Robert S. AUTO THEFT INVESTIGATION. Los Angeles, Calif.: Legal Book Corp., 1971.

580. Dexter, Lewis Anthony. ELITE AND SPECIALIZED INTERVIEWING. Evanston, Ill.: Northwestern University Press, 1970.

581. Dienstein, William. TECHNICS FOR THE CRIME INVESTIGATOR. Springfield, Ill.: Charles C. Thomas, 1972.

582. ELEMENTS OF INVESTIGATION. (16mm color, 14 min.) Sacramento, Calif.: California Peace Officers Association.

583. FOLLOW-UP INVESTIGATION. (Sound filmstrip, color.) Gaithersburg, Md.: International Association of Chiefs of Police.

584. Fraser, Gordon. MODERN TRANSPORTATION AND INTERNA-TIONAL CRIME. Springfield, Ill.: Charles C. Thomas, 1970.

585. GUIDE TO EVIDENCE COLLECTION. (Sound filmstrip, color.) Gaithersburg, Md.: International Association of Chiefs of Police.

586. GUIDELINES FOR INTERVIEWING. (Sound filmstrip, color.) Gaithersburg, Md.: International Association of Chiefs of Police.

587. Harney, Malachi L., and John C. Cross. THE INFORMER IN LAW ENFORCEMENT. Springfield, Ill.: Charles C. Thomas, 1968.

588. Inbau, Fred E., and John E. Reid. CRIMINAL INTERROGATION AND CONFESSIONS. Baltimore, Md.: Williams & Wilkins Co., 1967.

589. Inbau, Fred, and others. SCIENTIFIC POLICE INVESTIGATION. Philadelphia, Pa.: Chilton Book Co., 1972.

590. INFORMER. (Sound filmstrip, color.) Gaithersburg, Md.: Interna-tional Association of Chiefs of Police.

591. INVESTIGATING THE CRIME OF RAPE. (Sound filmstrip, color.) Gaithersburg, Md.: International Association of Chiefs of Police.

592. Kirk, Paul L. FIRE INVESTIGATION. New York, N.Y.: John Wiley and Sons, 1969.

★ 593. Leonard, V. A. CRIMINAL INVESTIGATION AND IDENTIFICA-TION. Springfield, Ill.: Charles C. Thomas, 1971.

★ 594. Leonard, V. A. THE POLICE DETECTIVE FUNCTION. Springfield, Ill.: Charles C. Thomas, 1970.

595. Motto, C. J. UNDERCOVER. Springfield, Ill.: Charles C. Thomas, 1971.

★ 596. O'Hara, Charles E. FUNDAMENTALS OF CRIMINAL INVESTIGA-TION. Springfield, Ill.: Charles C. Thomas, 1970.

597. Osterburg, James. THE CRIME LABORATORY: CASE STUDIES OF SCIENTIFIC CRIMINAL INVESTIGATION. Bloomington, Ind.: Indiana University Press, 1968.

598. Pollock, David. METHODS OF ELECTRONIC AUDIO SURVEIL-LANCE. Springfield, Ill.: Charles C. Thomas, 1972.

599. PRINCIPLES OF INVESTIGATION. (Sound filmstrip, color.) Gaithersburg, Md.: International Association of Chiefs of Police.

600. Ringel, William E. IDENTIFICATION AND POLICE LINE-UPS. Jamaica, N.Y.: Gould Publishing, 1968.

601. Ringel, William E. SEARCHES AND SEIZURES, ARRESTS AND CONFESSIONS. New York, N.Y.: Clark Boardman, 1972.

602. SEARCH AND SEIZURE. (Sound filmstrip, color.) Gaithersburg, Md.: International Association of Chiefs of Police.

603. SEARCHING THE CRIME SCENE. (16mm color, 20 min.) Washington, D.C.: Federal Bureau of Investigation.

604. Snyder, Lemoyne. HOMICIDE INVESTIGATION. Springfield, Ill.: Charles C. Thomas, 1967.

605. Specter, Arlen, and Marvin Katz. POLICE GUIDE TO SEARCH AND SEIZURE, INTERROGATION AND CONFESSION. Philadelphia, Pa.: Chilton Books, 1967.

606. Van Meter, C. H. PRINCIPLES OF POLICE INTERROGATION. Springfield, Ill.: Charles C. Thomas, 1973.

607. Vanderbosch, Charles G. CRIMINAL INVESTIGATION. Gaithersburg, Md.: International Association of Chiefs of Police, 1971.

★ 608. Weston, Paul, and Kenneth Wells. CRIMINAL INVESTIGATION: BASIC PERSPECTIVES. Englewood Cliffs, N.J.: Prentice Hall, 1970.

★ 609. Weston, Paul B. ELEMENTS OF CRIMINAL INVESTIGATION. Englewood Cliffs, N.J.: Prentice Hall, 1971.

610. WITNESS PERCEPTION. (Sound filmstrip, color.) Gaithersburg, Md.: International Association of Chiefs of Police.

See also Communications   Police Equipment
          Criminal Investigation   Police Patrol Function
          Criminology   Police Traffic Function
          Information: Systems/Software   Training

611. Bates, Bill. I.S.Q.D.—IDENTIFICATION SYSTEMS FOR QUES-
TIONED DOCUMENTS. Springfield, Ill.: Charles C. Thomas, 1970.

612. Bates, Bill. TYPEWRITING IDENTIFICATION I.S.Q.T.—IDENTIFI-
CATION SYSTEM FOR QUESTIONED TYPEWRITING. Springfield,
Ill.: Charles C. Thomas, 1971.

613. Block, Eugene B. FINGERPRINTING: MAGIC WEAPON AGAINST
CRIME. New York, N.Y.: David McKay, 1969.

614. Crown, David A. THE FORENSIC EXAMINATION OF PAINTS
AND PIGMENTS. Springfield, Ill.: Charles C. Thomas, 1968.

615. Curry, Alan. POISON DETECTION IN HUMAN ORGANS. Springfield, Ill.: Charles C. Thomas, 1969.

616. Ewing, Galen. INSTRUMENTAL METHODS OF CHEMICAL
ANALYSIS. New York, N.Y.: McGraw-Hill, 1969.

617. Ferguson, Robert J., Jr. THE SCIENTIFIC INFORMER. Springfield,
Ill.: Charles C. Thomas, 1971.

618. FINGERPRINTS. (Sound filmstrip, color.) Gaithersburg, Md.:
International Association of Chiefs of Police.

619. Fulton, Charles C. MODERN MICROCRYSTAL TESTS FOR DRUGS:
THE IDENTIFICATION OF ORGANIC COMPOUNDS BY MICRO-
CRYSTALLOSCOPIC CHEMISTRY. New York, N.Y.: John Wiley
and Sons, 1969.

620. Gleason, Marion N. CLINICAL TOXICOLOGY OF COMMERCIAL
PRODUCTS. Baltimore, Md.: Williams and Wilkins Co., 1969.

621. Kaye, Sidney. HANDBOOK OF EMERGENCY TOXICOLOGY.
Springfield, Ill.: Charles C. Thomas, 1970.

★ 622. Kirk, Paul L., and Lowell W. Bradford. THE CRIME LABORATORY:
ORGANIZATION AND OPERATION. Springfield, Ill.: Charles C.
Thomas, 1972.

623. Kroma, Vaclav. IDENTIFICATION AND REGISTRATION OF
FIREARMS. Springfield, Ill.: Charles C. Thomas, 1971.

624. LIE DETECTION. (Cassette tape, 27 min.) North Hollywood, Calif.: Center for Cassette Studies.

625. MacDonell, H. L. FLIGHT CHARACTERISTICS AND STAIN PATTERNS OF HUMAN BLOOD. Washington, D.C.: U. S. Government Printing Office, 1972.

626. Marcuse, Irene. GUIDE TO THE DISTURBED PERSONALITY THROUGH HANDWRITING. New York, N.Y.: Arco Publishing Co., 1969.

627. Middleton, Robert G. TROUBLESHOOTING WITH THE OSCILLO-SCOPE. Indianapolis, Ind.: Howard W. Sams and Co., 1967.

628. Moenssens, Andre A. FINGERPRINTS AND THE LAW. Philadelphia, Pa.: Chilton Books, 1969.

629. Moenssens, Andre A. FINGERPRINT TECHNIQUES. Philadelphia, Pa.: Chilton Books, 1971.

★ 630. O'Brien, Kevin, and Robert C. Sullivan. CRIMINALISTICS: THEORY AND PRACTICE. Boston, Mass.: Holbrook Press, 1972.

631. O'Hara, Charles, and James Osterburg. AN INTRODUCTION TO CRIMINALISTICS: THE APPLICATION OF THE PHYSICAL SCIENCES TO THE DETECTION OF CRIME. Bloomington, Ind.: Indiana University Press, 1972.

632. Olyanova, Nadya. HANDWRITING TELLS. Indianapolis, Ind.: Bobbs-Merrill Co., 1969.

633. Osterburg, James W. THE CRIME LABORATORY: CASE STUDIES OF SCIENTIFIC CRIMINAL INVESTIGATION. Bloomington, Ind.: Indiana University Press, 1968.

634. Picton, Bernard. MURDER, SUICIDE OR ACCIDENT: THE FORENSIC PATHOLOGIST AT WORK. Dunmore, Pa.: St. Martin's, 1971.

635. Polson, Cyril John, and D. J. Gee. ESSENTIALS OF FORENSIC MEDICINE. Elmsford, N.Y.: Pergamon Press, 1972.

636. Pountney, Harold. POLICE PHOTOGRAPHY. New York, N.Y.: American Elsevire Publishing Co., 1971.

637. Race, R. R., and Ruth Sanger. BLOOD GROUPS IN MAN. Philadelphia, Pa.: F. A. Davis Co., 1968.

638. Sansone, Sam J. MODERN PHOTOGRAPHY FOR POLICE AND FIREMEN. Cincinnati, Ohio: W. H. Anderson, 1971.

639. Sax, Newton. DANGEROUS PROPERTIES OF INDUSTRIAL MATERIALS. Cincinnati, Ohio: Van Nostrand Reinhold Co., 1968.

★ 640. Scott, Charles C. PHOTOGRAPHIC EVIDENCE: PREPARATION AND PRESENTATION (3 vols.). St. Paul, Minn.: West Publishing Co., 1967.

641. Sellers, B., and J. L. Hunerwadel. PROGRAM TO EXPLORE AND EVALUATE POTENTIAL APPLICATIONS OF RADIOISOTOPE EXCITED X-RAY FLUORESCENCE TECHNIQUES IN CRIMINALISTICS AND NATIONAL SECURITY. (Final Report.) Springfield, Va.: National Technical Information Service, 1969.

642. Simpson, Keith. FORENSIC MEDICINE. Baltimore, Md.: Williams and Wilkins Co., 1969.

643. Steere, Norman V. SAFETY IN THE CHEMICAL LABORATORY. Cleveland, Ohio: Chemical Rubber Publishing Co., 1967.

644. Sunshine, Irving. CRC MANUAL OF ANALYTICAL TOXICOLOGY. Cleveland, Ohio: Chemical Rubber Publishing Co., 1971.

645. Sussman, Leon. BLOOD GROUPING TESTS: MEDICO-LEGAL USES. Springfield, Ill.: Charles C. Thomas, 1968.

646. Telscher, Harry. HANDWRITING—REVELATION OF SELF: A SOURCEBOOK OF PSYCHOGRAPHOLOGY. New York, N.Y.: Hawthorn Books, 1971.

647. Tou, J. J. PICTORIAL PATTERN RECOGNITION—AUTOMATIC INTERPRETATION AND CLASSIFICATION OF FINGERPRINTS. Springfield, Va.: National Technical Information Service, 1970.

★ 648. Turner, William. INVISIBLE WITNESS: THE USE AND ABUSE OF THE NEW TECHNOLOGY OF CRIME INVESTIGATION. Indianapolis, Ind.: Bobbs-Merrill Co., 1968.

★ 649. U. S. Internal Revenue Service. FIREARMS IDENTIFICATION FOR LAW ENFORCEMENT OFFICERS. Washington, D.C.: U. S. Government Printing Office, 1970.

650. U. S. Law Enforcement Assistance Administration. CRIME LABORATORIES—THREE STUDY REPORTS. Springfield, Va.: National Technical Information Service, 1969.

651. U. S. Law Enforcement Assistance Administration. VOICE IDENTIFICATION RESEARCH. Washington, D.C.: U. S. Department of Justice, 1972.

652. U. S. Law Enforcement Assistance Administration. THE EXAMINA-
     TION AND TYPING OF BLOODSTAINS IN THE CRIME LABORA-
     TORY. Washington, D.C.: U. S. Government Printing Office, 1972.

★ 653. Walls, H. J. FORENSIC SCIENCE: AN INTRODUCTION TO THE
     SCIENCE OF CRIME DETECTION. New York, N.Y.: Praeger Pub-
     lishers, 1968.

654. Zavala, Albert, and James J. Paley (eds.). PERSONAL APPEARANCE
     IDENTIFICATION. Springfield, Ill.: Charles C. Thomas, 1972.

CRIMINOLOGY

See also Behavioral and Social Science
        Criminal Investigation
        Criminalistics
        Organized Crime
        Planning and Evaluation

Riot Control and Urban
   Disorders
Student Disorders
Support Services
Training
Victimless Crime

655. Bloch, Herbert, and Gilbert Geis. MAN, CRIME AND SOCIETY.
     Westminster, Md.: Random House, 1970.

656. Bonger, Willem. CRIMINALITY AND ECONOMIC CONDITIONS.
     Bloomington, Ind.: Indiana University Press, 1969.

657. Bromberg, Walter. CRIME AND THE MIND: AN OUTLINE OF
     PSYCHIATRIC CRIMINOLOGY. Westport, Conn.: Greenwood Press,
     1972.

658. Byrnes, Thomas. 1886 PROFESSIONAL CRIMINALS OF AMERICA.
     Westminster, Md.: Random House, 1969.

659. Casper, J. AMERICAN CRIMINAL JUSTICE: THE DEFENDENT'S
     PERSPECTIVE. Englewood Cliffs, N.J.: Prentice Hall, 1972.

660. Clark, Ramsey. CRIME IN AMERICA: ITS NATURE, CAUSES,
     CONTROL AND CORRECTION. New York, N.Y.: Simon and Schuster,
     1970.

★ 661. Clinard, Marshall. CRIMINAL BEHAVIOR SYSTEMS: A TYPOLOGY.
     New York, N.Y.: Holt, Rinehart and Winston, 1967.

662. Conrad, John. CRIME AND ITS CORRECTION. Berkeley, Calif.:
     University of California Press, 1967.

663. Cressey, Donald. CRIME AND CRIMINAL JUSTICE. Chicago, Ill.:
     Quadrangle Books, 1971.

664. CULTURE AND CRIMINAL ACTS. (Cassette tape, 27 min.) North Hollywood, Calif.: Center for Cassette Studies.

★ 665. Dinitz, Simon, and Walter C. Reckless. CRITICAL ISSUES IN THE STUDY OF CRIME: A BOOK OF READINGS. Boston, Mass.: Little, Brown and Co., 1968.

666. DiTullio, Benigno. HORIZONS IN CLINICAL CRIMINOLOGY. Hackensack, N.J.: Fred B. Rothman, 1969.

667. Dressler, David (ed.). READINGS IN CRIMINOLOGY AND PENOL-OGY. New York, N.Y.: Columbia University Press, 1972.

668. Ferri, Enrico. THE POSITIVE SCHOOL OF CRIMINOLOGY: THREE LECTURES. Pittsburgh, Pa.: University of Pittsburgh Press, 1968.

669. Gibbons, Don C. SOCIETY, CRIME AND CRIMINAL CAREERS: AN INTRODUCTION TO CRIMINOLOGY. Englewood Cliffs, N.J.: Prentice Hall, 1968.

670. Glaser, Daniel. ADULT CRIME AND SOCIAL POLICY. Englewood Cliffs, N.J.: Prentice Hall, 1972.

★ 671. Glaser, Daniel (ed.). CRIME IN THE CITY. New York, N.Y.: Harper and Row, 1970.

672. Grupp, Stanley E. THE POSITIVE SCHOOL OF CRIMINOLOGY. Pittsburgh, Pa.: University of Pittsburgh Press, 1968.

★ 673. Guenther, Anthony L. CRIMINAL BEHAVIOR AND SOCIAL SYSTEMS: CONTRIBUTIONS OF AMERICAN SOCIOLOGY. Chicago, Ill.: Rand McNally, 1970.

674. HEREDITARY CRIMINAL. (Cassette tape, 26 min.) North Hollywood, Calif.: Center for Cassette Studies.

★ 675. Hood, Roger, and Richard Sparks. KEY ISSUES IN CRIMINOLOGY. New York, N.Y.: McGraw-Hill, 1970.

676. Hughes, Helen MacGill (comp.). DELINQUENTS AND CRIMINALS: THEIR SOCIAL WORLD. Boston, Mass.: Holbrook Press, 1972.

677. Jackson, Bruce. A THIEF'S PRIMER: LIFE OF AN AMERICAN CHARACTER. Riverside, N.J.: Macmillan Co., 1969.

678. Jeffers, Harry. WANTED BY THE F.B.I. New York, N.Y.: Hawthorn Books, 1972.

★ 679.   Jeffery, C. R. CRIMINAL RESPONSIBILITY AND MENTAL
         DISEASE. Springfield, Ill.: Charles C. Thomas, 1967.

  680.   Johnson, Elmer Hubert. CRIME, CORRECTIONS, AND SOCIETY.
         Homewood, Ill.: Dorsey Press, 1968.

  681.   Joint Commission on Corrections, Manpower and Training. THE
         PUBLIC LOOKS AT CRIME AND CORRECTIONS. Washington, D.C.:
         American Correctional Association, 1968.

  682.   Kampa, Leo. THE ENIGMA OF CRIME. Philadelphia, Pa.: Dorrance
         and Co., 1972.

  683.   Klein, Malcolm. STREET GANGS AND STREET WORKERS.
         Englewood Cliffs, N.J.: Prentice Hall, 1971.

★ 684.   Knudten, Richard D. CRIME, CRIMINOLOGY, AND CONTEMPOR-
         ARY SOCIETY. Homewood, Ill.: Dorsey Press, 1970.

★ 685.   Knudten, Richard D. CRIME IN A COMPLEX SOCIETY: AN
         INTRODUCTION TO CRIMINOLOGY. Homewood, Ill.: Dorsey Press,
         1970.

  686.   Knudten, Richard D. CRIMINOLOGICAL CONTROVERSIES. New
         York, N.Y.: Appleton Century Croft, 1968.

  687.   Leinwand, Gerald. CRIME AND JUVENILE DELINQUENCY:
         PROBLEMS OF AMERICAN SOCIETY. New York, N.Y.: Washington
         Square Press, 1968.

★ 688.   Lipton, Dean. THE FACES OF CRIME AND GENIUS: THE HISTOR-
         ICAL IMPACT OF THE GENIUS CRIMINAL. South Brunswick,
         N.J.: A. S. Barnes, 1970.

  689.   Lopez-Ray, Manuel. CRIME, AN ANALYTICAL APPRAISAL. New
         York, N.Y.: Praeger Publishers, 1970.

  690.   Lunden, Walter A. CRIMES AND CRIMINALS. Ames, Iowa: Iowa
         State University Press, 1967.

★ 691.   Mayo, Patricia Elton. THE MAKING OF A CRIMINAL. New York,
         N.Y.: Universe Books, 1970.

  692.   Mays, John Barron. CRIME AND ITS TREATMENT. New York,
         N.Y.: Humanities Press, 1970.

★ 693.   McLennan, Barbara N. (ed.). CRIME IN URBAN SOCIETY. New
         York, N.Y.: Dunellen Publishing Co., 1970.

694. Menninger, Karl. CRIME OF PUNISHMENT. New York, N.Y.: Viking Press, 1968.

695. Morland, Nigel. AN OUTLINE OF SCIENTIFIC CRIMINOLOGY. New York, N.Y.: St. Martin's Press, 1971.

★ 696. Mueller, Gerhard O. W. CRIME, LAW AND THE SCHOLARS: A HISTORY OF SCHOLARSHIP IN AMERICAN CRIMINAL LAW. Seattle, Wash.: University of Washington Press, 1969.

★ 697. Packer, Herbert L. THE LIMITS OF THE CRIMINAL SANCTION. Stanford, Calif.: Stanford University Press, 1968.

698. Parsons, Philip A. RESPONSIBILITY FOR CRIME: AN INVESTI-GATION OF THE NATURE AND CAUSES OF CRIME AND A MEANS OF ITS PREVENTION. New York, N.Y.: AMS Press, 1968.

★ 699. President's Commission on Law Enforcement and Administration of Justice. THE CHALLENGE OF CRIME IN A FREE SOCIETY: FINAL REPORT. Washington, D.C.: U. S. Government Printing Office, 1967.

★ 700. President's Commission on Law Enforcement and Administration of Justice. CRIME AND ITS IMPACT—AN ASSESSMENT: TASK FORCE REPORT. Washington, D.C.: U. S. Government Printing Office, 1967.

701. Quinney, Richard (ed.). CRIME AND JUSTICE IN SOCIETY. Boston, Mass.: Little, Brown and Co., 1969.

702. Quinney, Richard. THE PROBLEM OF CRIME. New York, N.Y.: Dodd, Mead & Co., 1970.

703. Quinney, Richard. THE SOCIAL REALITY OF CRIME. Waltham, Mass.: Little, Brown and Co., 1970.

704. Radzinowicz, Leon (ed.). CRIME AND JUSTICE. (3 vols.) New York, N.Y.: Basic Books, 1971.

705. RAMSEY CLARK ON CRIME. (Cassette tape, 51 min.) North Hollywood, Calif.: Center for Cassette Studies.

706. Reasons, Charles, and Jack Kuykendall (eds.). RACE, CRIME, AND JUSTICE. Palisades, Calif.: Goodyear Publishing Co., 1971.

★ 707. Reckless, Walter C. THE CRIME PROBLEM. New York, N.Y.: Appleton Century Crofts, 1967.

708. Reynolds, M. O. CRIMES FOR PROFIT: ECONOMICS OF THEFT. Ann Arbor, Mich.: University Microfilm, 1970.

★ 709. Roebuck, Julian B. CRIMINAL TYPOLOGY. Springfield, Ill.: Charles C. Thomas, 1967.

★ 710. Savitz, Leonard. DILEMMAS IN CRIMINOLOGY. New York, N.Y.: McGraw-Hill, 1967.

★ 711. Schafer, Stephen. THEORIES IN CRIMINOLOGY: PAST AND PRESENT PHILOSOPHIES OF THE CRIME PROBLEM. Westminster, Md.: Random House, 1969.

712. Schafer, Stephen. THE VICTIM AND HIS CRIMINAL: A STUDY IN FUNCTIONAL RESPONSIBILITY. Westminster, Md.: Random House, 1968.

713. Schafer, Stephen. THE VICTIM AND HIS CRIMINAL—VICTIMOL-OGY. (President's Committee on Law Enforcement and the Administration of Justice.) Washington, D.C.: U. S. Government Printing Office, 1967.

714. Schur, Edwin. OUR CRIMINAL SOCIETY: THE SOCIAL AND LEGAL SOURCES OF CRIME IN AMERICA. Englewood Cliffs, N.J.: Prentice Hall, 1969.

715. Shoham, Shlomo. THE MARK OF CAIN. Dobbs Ferry, N.Y.: Oceana Publishers, 1970.

716. Silving, Helen. CONSTITUENT ELEMENTS OF CRIME. Springfield, Ill.: Charles C. Thomas, 1967.

717. Silving, Helen. ESSAYS ON MENTAL INCAPACITY AND CRIMI-NAL CONDUCT. Springfield, Ill.: Charles C. Thomas, 1967.

718. Smart, Frances, and Beatrice Brown. NEUROSIS AND CRIME. Scranton, Pa.: Barnes and Noble, 1970.

719. Smigel, Erwin O., and Hugh L. Ross. CRIMES AGAINST BUREAU-CRACY. Cincinnati, Ohio: Van Nostrand Reinhold Co., 1970.

★ 720. Sutherland, Edwin H., and Donald R. Cressey. CRIMINOLOGY. Philadelphia, Pa.: J. B. Lippincott Co., 1970.

721. Sykes, Gresham M. CRIME AND SOCIETY. Westminster, Md.: Random House, 1967.

722. Sykes, Gresham, and Thomas Drabek. LAW AND THE LAWLESS: A READER IN CRIMINOLOGY. Westminster, Md.: Random House, 1969.

723. U. S. Center for Studies in Crime and Delinquency. National Institute of Mental Health. CRIME AND JUSTICE—AMERICAN STYLE. Washington, D.C.: U. S. Government Printing Office, 1971.

724. U. S. Chamber of Commerce. MARSHALING CITIZEN POWER AGAINST CRIME. Washington, D.C.: Chamber of Commerce of United States, 1970.

725. VICTIM OF CRIME. (Cassette tape, 50 min.) North Hollywood, Calif.: Center for Cassette Studies.

726. Voss, Harwin. ECOLOGY, CRIME, AND DELINQUENCY. New York, N.Y.: Appleton Century Croft, 1971.

727. Westley, William. VIOLENCE AND THE POLICE: A SOCIOLOGICAL STUDY OF LAW, CUSTOM AND MORALITY. Cambridge, Mass.: Massachusetts Institute of Technology Press, 1970.

728. Wolfgang, Marvin E. CRIME AND CULTURE: ESSAYS IN HONOR OF THORSTEN SELLIN. New York, N.Y.: John Wiley and Sons, 1968.

729. Wolfgang, Marvin E. STUDIES IN HOMICIDE. New York, N.Y.: Harper and Row, 1967.

730. Wolfgang, Marvin E., and Bernard Cohen. CRIME AND RACE: CONCEPTIONS AND MISCONCEPTIONS. New York, N.Y.: Institute of Human Relations, 1970.

731. Wolfgang, Marvin, and others. THE SOCIOLOGY OF CRIME AND DELINQUENCY. New York, N.Y.: John Wiley and Sons, 1970.

DOMESTIC RELATIONS

See also **Behavioral and Social Science**   **Juvenile Delinquency**
Community Relations   **Support Services**
Criminology

732. Abrahams, Samuel. LAW IN FAMILY CONFLICT. New York, N.Y.: Law-Arts Publishing Co., 1970.

733. Evans, M. Stanton, and Margaret Moore. THE LAWBREAKERS: AMERICA'S NUMBER ONE DOMESTIC PROBLEM. New Rochelle, N.Y.: Arlington House, 1968.

734. Fishbein, Morris, and Justin Fishbein (eds.). SUCCESSFUL MARRIAGE: A MODERN GUIDE TO LOVE, SEX AND FAMILY LIFE. Garden City, N.Y.: Doubleday and Co., 1971.

735. Group for the Advancement of Psychiatry. TREATMENT OF FAMILIES IN CONFLICT: THE CLINICAL STUDY OF FAMILY PROCESS. New York, N.Y.: Science House Ltd., 1970.

736. Kriesberg, Louis. MOTHERS IN POVERTY: A STUDY OF FATHERLESS FAMILIES. Chicago, Ill.: Aldine/Atherton, 1970.

737. Minuchin, Salvador, and others. FAMILIES OF THE SLUMS: AN EXPLORATION OF THEIR STRUCTURE AND TREATMENT. New York, N.Y.: Basic Books, 1967.

738. Mowrer, Ernest. FAMILY DISORGANIZATION: AN INTRODUCTION TO SOCIOLOGICAL ANALYSIS. New York, N.Y.: Arno Press, 1972.

739. Pollak, Otto, and Alfred S. Friedman. FAMILY DYNAMICS AND SEXUAL DELINQUENCY. Palo Alto, Calif.: Science and Behavior Books, 1968.

★ 740. Rainwater, Lee. BEHIND GHETTO WALLS: BLACK FAMILY LIFE IN A FEDERAL SLUM. Chicago, Ill.: Aldine/Atherton, 1970.

741. Richette, Lisa Aversa. THE THROWAWAY CHILDREN. Philadelphia, Pa.: J. B. Lippincott, 1969.

742. Schlesinger, Benjamin. THE ONE-PARENT FAMILY: PERSPECTIVES AND ANNOTATED BIBLIOGRAPHY. Buffalo, N.Y.: University of Toronto Press, 1970.

743. Stuart, Irving, and Lawrence Abt. CHILDREN OF SEPARATION AND DIVORCE. New York, N.Y.: Grossman, 1972.

744. Szurek, S. A., and I. N. Berlin (eds.). THE ANTISOCIAL CHILD: HIS FAMILY AND HIS COMMUNITY. Palo Alto, Calif.: Science and Behavior Books, 1969.

See also Behavioral and Social Science
Criminology
Judicial Process
Juvenile Delinquency

Laws and Statutes
Organized Crime
Support Service
Victimless Crime

745. Aaronson, Bernard. PSYCHEDELICS: THE USES AND IMPLICA-
TIONS OF HALLUCINOGENIC DRUGS. Garden City, N.Y.: Anchor
Books, 1970.

746. Alexander, Clifton A., and Sandy Alexander. HOW TO KICK THE
HABIT: A GUIDE TO DRUG WITHDRAWAL. New York, N.Y.: Fell,
1972.

747. Ball, John, and Carl Chambers. THE EPIDEMIOLOGY OF OPIATE
ADDICTION IN THE UNITED STATES. Springfield, Ill.: Charles C.
Thomas, 1970.

★ 748. Barber, Bernard. DRUGS AND SOCIETY. New York, N.Y.: Russell
Sage Foundation, 1967.

749. Barber, Theodore Xenophen. L.S.D., MARIHUANA, YOGA, AND
HYPNOSIS. Chicago, Ill.: Aldine/Atherton, 1970.

750. Baskin, Esther, and Leonard Baskin. THE POPPY AND OTHER
DEADLY PLANTS. New York, N.Y.: Dell Publishing Co., 1967.

751. Bejerot, Nils. ADDICTION AND SOCIETY. Springfield, Ill.: Charles
C. Thomas, 1970.

752. Bennett, James C., and George D. Demes. DRUG ABUSE AND WHAT
WE CAN DO ABOUT IT. Springfield, Ill.: Charles C. Thomas, 1972.

753. Blachly, Paul. DRUG ABUSE DATA AND DEBATE. Springfield,
Ill.: Charles C. Thomas, 1970.

754. Blakeslee, Alton. WHAT YOU SHOULD KNOW ABOUT DRUGS
AND NARCOTICS. New York, N.Y.: Associated Press, 1969.

755. Bludworth, Edward. THREE HUNDRED MOST ABUSED DRUGS.
Tampa, Fla.: Trend Publications, 1972.

756. Blum, Richard. SOCIETY AND DRUGS: SOCIAL AND CULTURAL
OBSERVATIONS. San Francisco, Calif.: Jossey-Bass, 1969.

757. Braceland, Francis, and others. DRUG ABUSE: MEDICAL AND
CRIMINAL ASPECTS. New York, N.Y.: MSS Information Corp,
1972.

★ 758. Brill, Leon, and Ernest Harms (eds.). THE YEARBOOK OF DRUG
         ABUSE. New York, N.Y.: Behavioral Publications, 1972.

  759. Brotman, Richard. A COMMUNITY MENTAL HEALTH APPROACH
         TO DRUG ADDICTION. Washington, D.C.: National Education
         Association, 1968.

  760. Clarke, E. G. ISOLATION AND IDENTIFICATION OF DRUGS.
         Philadelphia, Pa.: Pharmaceutical Press, 1968.

★ 761. Cole, Jonathan O., and J. Richard Wittenborn. DRUG ABUSE:
         SOCIAL AND PSYCHOPHARMACOLOGICAL ASPECTS. Springfield,
         Ill.: Charles C. Thomas, 1970.

  762. Coles, Robert, and others. DRUGS AND YOUTH: MEDICAL,
         PSYCHIATRIC AND LEGAL FACTS. New York, N.Y.: Avon Books,
         1971.

★ 763. Debold, Richard C. LSD: MAN AND SOCIETY. Middletown, Conn.:
         Wesleyan University Press, 1967.

★ 764. Eldridge, William Butler. NARCOTICS AND THE LAW: A CRITIQUE
         OF THE AMERICAN EXPERIMENT IN NARCOTIC DRUG CON-
         TROL. Chicago, Ill.: University of Chicago Press, 1967.

  765. Evans, Wayne. PSYCHOTROPIC DRUGS IN THE YEAR 2000: USE
         BY NORMAL HUMANS. Springfield, Ill.: Charles C. Thomas, 1971.

  766. Falconer, Mary, and others. CURRENT DRUG HANDBOOK 1972-74.
         Philadelphia, Pa.: W. B. Saunders, 1972.

  767. Fiddle, Seymour. PORTRAIT FROM A SHOOTING GALLERY:
         LIFE STYLES FROM THE DRUG ADDICT WORLD. New York, N.Y.:
         Harper and Row, 1967.

  768. FIGHT OR FLIGHT. (16mm color, 15 min.) Gaithersburg, Md.:
         International Association of Chiefs of Police.

  769. Fort, Joel. THE PLEASURE SEEKERS: THE DRUG CRISIS, YOUTH
         AND SOCIETY. Indianapolis, Ind.: Bobbs-Merrill Co., 1969.

  770. Geller, Allen, and Maxwell Boas. THE DRUG BEAT. New York, N.Y.:
         McGraw-Hill, 1969.

  771. Gitchoff, G. Thomas. KIDS, COPS, AND KILOS: A STUDY OF CON-
         TEMPORARY SUBURBAN YOUTH. San Diego, Calif.: Malter-
         Westerfield Co., 1969.

772. Goldhill, Paul. PARENT'S GUIDE TO THE PREVENTION AND CONTROL OF DRUG ABUSE. Chicago, Ill.: Henry Regnery Co., 1971.

773. Goode, Erich. MARIJUANA. Chicago, Ill.: Atherton Press, 1969.

774. Goode, Erich. THE MARIJUANA SMOKERS. New York, N.Y.: Basic Books, 1970.

775. Grinspoon, Lester. MARIHUANA RECONSIDERED. Cambridge, Mass.: Harvard University Press, 1971.

776. Gustaitis, Rasa. TURNING ON. Riverside, N.J.: Macmillan Co., 1968.

777. Hafen, Brent. READINGS ON DRUG USE AND ABUSE. Provo, Utah: Brigham Young University Press, 1970.

778. Hart, Harold. DRUGS: FOR AND AGAINST. New York, N.Y.: Hart Publishing Co., 1970.

779. Healy, Patrick, and James Manak (eds.). DRUG DEPENDENCE AND ABUSE RESOURCE BOOK. Chicago, Ill.: National District Attorneys Association, 1971.

780. Hemsing, Esther. CHILDREN AND DRUGS. Washington, D.C.: Association for Childhood Education International, 1972.

781. Hentoff, Nat. A DOCTOR AMONG THE ADDICTS. Chicago, Ill.: Rand McNally, 1968.

782. Hollister, Leo. CHEMICAL PSYCHOSES: LSD AND RELATED DRUGS. Springfield, Ill.: Charles C. Thomas, 1968.

783. Hyde, Margaret O. MIND DRUGS. New York, N.Y.: McGraw-Hill, 1968.

784. Jones, Kenneth Lester, and others. DRUGS, ALCOHOL, AND TOBACCO. New York, N.Y.: Harper and Row, 1970.

785. Kaplan, John. MARIJUANA—THE NEW PROHIBITION. Cleveland, Ohio: World Publishing Co., 1970.

786. Kaplan, Robert. DRUG ABUSE: PERSPECTIVES ON DRUGS. Dubuque, Iowa: William C. Brown Co., 1970.

787. KEEP OFF THE GRASS. (16mm color, 20 min.) Los Angeles, Calif.: Sid Davis Productions.

788. Konnor, Delbert D. (ed.). DRUG ADDICTION AND HABITUA-
      TION. Detroit, Mich.: Wayne State University Press, 1968.

789. Laurie, Peter. DRUGS: MEDICAL, PSYCHOLOGICAL AND SOCIAL
      FACTS. Sante Fe, New Mex.: Gannon, 1967.

790. Leech, Kenneth, and B. Jordan. DRUGS FOR YOUNG PEOPLE.
      Elmsford, N.Y.: Pergamon Press, 1967.

791. Lennard, Henry. MYSTIFICATION AND DRUG MISUSE: HAZARDS
      IN USING PSYCHOACTIVE DRUGS. San Francisco, Calif.: Jossey-
      Bass, 1971.

792. Lindesmith, Alfred. ADDICTION AND OPIATES. Chicago, III.:
      Aldine/Atherton, 1968.

793. Lord, Jess. MARIJUANA AND PERSONALITY CHANGE. Lexington,
      Mass.: Lexington Books, 1971.

794. Louria, Donald B. THE DRUG SCENE. New York, N.Y.: McGraw-
      Hill, 1968.

795. Maddox, George L. (ed.). THE DOMESTICATED DRUG. New Haven,
      Conn.: College and University Press, 1970.

796. MARIJUANA—THE GREAT ESCAPE. (16mm color, 20 min.) Santa
      Monica, Calif.: BFA Educational Media.

797. Marriott, Alice, and Carol K. Rachlin. PEYOTE. New York, N.Y.:
      Thomas Y. Crowell Co., 1971.

798. Maurer, David W., and Victor H. Vogel. NARCOTICS AND NAR-
      COTIC ADDICTION. Springfield, III.: Charles C. Thomas, 1971.

799. McGrath, John H. YOUTH AND DRUGS: PERSPECTIVES ON A
      SOCIAL PROBLEM. Oakland, N.J.: Scott Foresman and Co., 1970.

800. Meyer, Roger. GUIDE TO DRUG REHABILITATION. Boston, Mass.:
      Beacon Press, 1972.

801. NARCOSIS. (16mm color, 24 min.) Sacramento, Calif.: California
      Peace Officers Association.

802. Nowlis, Helen H. DRUGS ON THE COLLEGE CAMPUS. Garden City,
      N.Y.: Doubleday and Co., 1968.

★ 803. Oursler, Will. MARIJUANA: THE FACTS—THE TRUTH. New York,
      N.Y.: Paul S. Eriksson, 1970.

804. Pace, Denny, and Jimmy Styles. HANDBOOK ON NARCOTICS CONTROL. Englewood Cliffs, N.J.: Prentice Hall, 1972.

805. THE PILL POPPERS. (16mm color, 20 min.) Los Angeles, Calif.: Sid Davis Productions.

★ 806. President's Commission on Law Enforcement and Administration of Justice. NARCOTICS AND DRUG ABUSE: TASK FORCE REPORT. Washington, D.C.: U.S. Government Printing Office, 1967.

807. RECOGNITION OF DRUGS. (Sound filmstrip, color.) Gaithersburg, Md.: International Association of Chiefs of Police.

808. Russo, J. Robert. AMPHETAMINE ABUSE. Springfield, Ill.: Charles C. Thomas, 1968.

★ 809. Scott, Edward. THE ADOLESCENT GAP: RESEARCH FINDINGS ON DRUG USING AND NON-DRUG USING TEENS. Springfield, Ill.: Charles C. Thomas, 1971.

810. Scott, J. M. THE WHITE POPPY. New York, N.Y.: Funk and Wagnalls Co., 1969.

811. Seymour, Whitney. YOUNG DIE QUIETLY: THE NARCOTICS PROBLEM IN AMERICA. New York, N.Y.: William Morrow, 1972.

812. Smith, David E. THE NEW SOCIAL DRUG: CULTURAL, MEDICAL AND LEGAL PERSPECTIVES ON MARIJUANA. Englewood Cliffs, N.J.: Prentice Hall, 1970.

813. Smith, David, and George R. Gay (eds.). IT'S SO GOOD, DON'T EVEN TRY IT ONCE: HEROIN IN PERSPECTIVE. Englewood Cliffs, N.J.: Prentice Hall, 1972.

814. Snyder, Solomon H. USES OF MARIJUANA. New York, N.Y.: Oxford University Press, 1971.

★ 815. U.S. Bureau of Narcotics and Dangerous Drugs. GUIDELINES FOR DRUG ABUSE AND PREVENTION EDUCATION. Washington, D.C.: U.S. Bureau of Narcotics and Dangerous Drugs, 1970.

816. U.S. Bureau of Narcotics and Dangerous Drugs. PUBLIC SPEAKING ON DRUG ABUSE PREVENTION: A HANDBOOK FOR THE LAW ENFORCEMENT OFFICER. Washington, D.C.: U.S. Government Printing Office, 1970.

817. U.S. Congress (House) Select Committee on Crime. AMPHETA-MINES: FOURTH REPORT. Washington, D.C.: U.S. Government Printing Office, 1971.

818. U. S. Congress (House) Select Committee on Crime. MARIJUANA: FIRST REPORT. Washington, D.C.: U. S. Government Printing Office, 1970.

819. U. S. Congress (Senate). DRUG ABUSE PREVENTION AND CON-TROL. Washington, D.C.: U. S. Government Printing Office, 1972.

820. U. S. Congress (Senate). NARCOTICS AND ALCOHOLISM. Washington, D.C.: U. S. Government Printing Office, 1971.

821. U.S. Department of Health, Education and Welfare. DRUGS AND YOUR BODY. Washington, D.C.: American Association for Health, 1968.

822. U. S. Department of Health, Education and Welfare. NARCOTICS: SOME QUESTIONS AND ANSWERS. Washington, D.C.: U. S. Government Printing Office, 1968.

823. U. S. Law Enforcement Assistance Administration. LEAA DRUG ABUSE PROGRAM. Washington, D.C.: U. S. Law Enforcement Assistance Administration, 1971.

824. U. S. National Clearinghouse for Drug Abuse Information. A FEDERAL SOURCE BOOK: ANSWERS TO THE MOST FREQUENTLY ASKED QUESTIONS ABOUT DRUG ABUSE. Washington, D.C.: U. S. Government Printing Office, 1970.

825. U. S. National Commission on Marijuana and Drug Abuse. MARI-JUANA: A SIGNAL OF MISUNDERSTANDING—FIRST REPORT. Washington, D.C.: U. S. Government Printing Office, 1972.

826. U. S. National Institute of Mental Health. DON'T GUESS ABOUT DRUGS WHEN YOU CAN HAVE THE FACTS. Washington, D.C.: U. S. Government Printing Office, 1970.

★ 827. U. S. National Institute of Mental Health. RECENT RESEARCH ON NARCOTICS, LSD, MARIHUANA AND OTHER DANGEROUS DRUGS. Washington, D.C.: U. S. Government Printing Office, 1970.

828. U. S. National Institute of Mental Health. RESOURCE BOOK FOR DRUG ABUSE EDUCATION. Washington, D.C.: National Education Association, 1969.

829. U. S. National Institute of Mental Health. STUDENTS AND DRUG ABUSE. Washington, D.C.: U. S. Government Printing Office, 1969.

830. U. S. Youth Development and Delinquency Prevention Administra-tion. YOUTHFUL DRUG USE. Washington, D.C.: U. S. Government Printing Office, 1970.

831. Westman, Wesley. PROGRAMMED LEARNING AID FOR BASIC FACTS ON DRUG ABUSE. Homewood, Ill.: Learning Systems Co., 1972.

832. Williams, John B. (ed.). NARCOTICS AND HALLUCINOGENICS: HANDBOOK. Riverside, N.J.: Glencoe Press, 1967.

★ 833. Wittenborn, J. R., and others. DRUGS AND YOUTH. Springfield, Ill.: Charles C. Thomas, 1969.

834. Zinberg, Norman, and John Robertson. DRUGS AND THE PUBLIC. New York, N.Y.: Simon and Schuster, 1972.

835. Zwerin, Michael. THE SILENT SOUND OF NEEDLES. Englewood Cliffs, N.J.: Prentice Hall, 1969.

EDUCATION

See also **Personnel Administration** **Research and Development**
Planning and Evaluation **Security Systems**
Public Information and Education **Support Services**
Reference Material **Training**

836. Cowles Book Company. THE COWLES CLEP BOOK: PREPARATION FOR THE COLLEGE LEVEL EXAMINATION PROGRAM: GENERAL EXAMINATIONS. Chicago, Ill.: Cowles Book Co., 1970.

837. Cowles Book Company. COWLES GED PROGRAM: PREPARATION FOR THE HIGH SCHOOL EQUIVALENCY EXAMINATION (GED). Chicago, Ill.: Cowles Book Co., 1972.

★ 838. Crockett, Thompson. A SURVEY AND DISCUSSION OF LAW ENFORCEMENT EDUCATION IN THE UNITED STATES. Gaithersburg, Md.: International Association of Chiefs of Police, 1968.

839. Ehrlich, Eugene H. HOW TO STUDY BETTER AND GET HIGHER MARKS. New York, N.Y.: Apollo Editions, 1969.

840. Johnson, Ellsworth, K. O. Price, and Lloyd Kent. POLICE TRAINING IN A CHANGING SOCIETY. Los Angeles, Calif.: University of Southern California, 1967.

841. Lejins, P. P. INTRODUCING A LAW ENFORCEMENT CURRICULUM AT A STATE UNIVERSITY. Washington, D.C.: U. S. Government Printing Office, 1970.

842. Saunders, Charles. UPGRADING THE AMERICAN POLICE: EDUCA-
     TION AND TRAINING FOR BETTER LAW ENFORCEMENT.
     Washington, D.C.: Brookings Institute, 1970.

843. Thorndike, Robert, and others. EDUCATIONAL MEASUREMENT.
     Washington, D.C.: American Council on Education, 1971.

★ 844. U. S. Law Enforcement Assistance Administration. HIGHER EDUCA-
     TION PROGRAMS IN LAW ENFORCEMENT AND CRIMINAL
     JUSTICE. Washington, D.C.: U. S. Government Printing Office, 1972.

EXPLOSIVES AND WEAPONS

See also **Crime Deterrence and**   **Police Equipment**
          Prevention   **Riots and Urban Disorders**
          Organized Crime   **Training**

845. BOMBS I, II, III. (16mm or videotape, color, 20 min. each) Chicago,
     Ill.: Motorola Systems, Inc.

846. Brodle, Thomas. BOMBS AND BOMBING: A HANDBOOK TO
     DETECTION, DISPOSAL AND INVESTIGATION—FOR POLICE
     AND FIRE DEPARTMENTS. Springfield, Ill.: Charles C. Thomas,
     1972.

847. Lenz, Robert. EXPLOSIVES AND BOMB DISPOSAL GUIDE.
     Springfield, Ill.: Charles C. Thomas, 1971.

★ 848. Powell, William. THE ANARCHIST COOKBOOK. New York, N.Y.:
     Lyle Stuart Publisher, 1971.

849. Stoffel, Joseph F. EXPLOSIVES AND HOMEMADE BOMBS. Spring-
     field, Ill.: Charles C. Thomas, 1972.

★ 850. U.S. National Commission on Prevention of Violence. FIRE-
     ARMS AND VIOLENCE IN AMERICAN LIFE. Washington,
     D.C.: U.S. Government Printing Office, 1969.

INFORMATION SYSTEMS/SOFTWARE

See also **Communications: Data/Visual/**   **Police Equipment**
          Voice/Equipment

851. Armour, David, and A. S. Couch. DATA-TEXT PRIMER: AN INTRO-
     DUCTION TO COMPUTERIZED SOCIAL DATA ANALYSIS.
     New York, N.Y.: Free Press, 1972.

852. Avedon, Donald. COMPUTER OUTPUT MICROFILM. Silver Springs, Md.: National Microfilm Association, 1971.

853. Brightman, Richard. INFORMATION SYSTEMS FOR MODERN MANAGEMENT. Riverside, N.J.: Macmillan Co., 1971.

854. Brown, John A. COMPUTERS AND AUTOMATION. New York, N.Y.: Arco Publishing Co., 1968.

855. Director, Stephen. INTRODUCTION TO SYSTEMS THEORY. New York, N.Y.: McGraw-Hill, 1972.

856. Gauthier, Richard, and Stephen Ponto. DESIGNING SYSTEMS PROGRAMS. Englewood Cliffs, N.J.: Prentice Hall, 1970.

857. Gruenberger, Fred. COMPUTER GRAPHICS: UTILITY, PRODUC-TION, ART. Narberth, Pa.: Psychonetics, 1967.

858. Gruenberger, Fred. COMPUTING: AN INTRODUCTION. New York, N.Y.: Harcourt Brace Jovanovich, 1969.

★ 859. Hansen, David A., and John J. Kolbmann. CLOSED CIRCUIT TELEVISION FOR POLICE. Springfield, Ill.: Charles C. Thomas, 1970.

860. Harrell, T., and others. HANDBOOK OF DATA PROCESSING MANAGEMENT. Boston, Mass.: Brandon/Systems Press, 1970.

861. Kanter, Jerome. MANAGEMENT-ORIENTED MANAGEMENT INFORMATION SYSTEMS. Englewood Cliffs, N.J.: Prentice Hall, 1972.

862. Krauss, Leonard J. ADMINISTERING AND CONTROLLING THE COMPANY DATA PROCESSING FUNCTION. Englewood Cliffs, N.J.: Prentice Hall, 1969.

863. LeBreton, Preston. ADMINISTRATIVE INTELLIGENCE— INFORMATION SYSTEMS. Boston, Mass.: Houghton Mifflin Co., 1969.

864. Marill, T. CYCLOPS SYSTEM RESEARCH: FINAL REPORT. Springfield, Va.: National Technical Information Service, 1970.

865. Matthews, Don. THE DESIGN OF THE MANAGEMENT INFORMA-TION SYSTEM. Princeton, N.J.: Auerbach, 1971.

866. Prince, Lawrence, and David Nyman. INTRODUCTION TO COMPUTERS AND COMPUTER PROGRAMMING. Englewood Cliffs, N.J.: Prentice Hall, 1972.

★ 867. Rieder, Robert J. LAW ENFORCEMENT INFORMATION SYSTEMS. Springfield, Ill.: Charles C. Thomas, 1972.

868. Sharpe, William. THE ECONOMICS OF COMPUTERS. Irvington, N.Y.: Columbia University Press, 1969.

869. Sisson, Roger L., and R. G. Canning. A MANAGER'S GUIDE TO COMPUTER PROCESSING. New York, N.Y.: John Wiley and Sons, 1967.

870. U. S. Housing and Urban Development Department. URBAN AND REGIONAL INFORMATION SYSTEMS: SUPPORT FOR PLANNING IN METROPOLITAN AREAS. Washington, D.C.: U. S. Government Printing Office, 1969.

871. Wadsworth, M. D. EDP PROJECT MANAGEMENT CONTROLS. Englewood Cliffs, N.J.: Prentice Hall, 1972.

★ 872. Whisenand, Paul M. AUTOMATED POLICE INFORMATION SYSTEMS. New York, N.Y.: John Wiley and Sons, 1970.

JAILS

See also **Community Based Corrections:**   **Judicial Process**
        Adult/Juvenile   **Laws and Statutes**
        Correctional Institutions: **Probation and Parole:**
        Adult/Juvenile   **Adult/Juvenile**

★ 873. Pappas, Nick. THE JAIL—ITS OPERATION AND MANAGEMENT. Washington, D.C.: U. S. Bureau of Prisons, 1971.

874. U. S. Bureau of Prisons. CLASSIFICATION OF JAIL PRISONERS. Washington, D.C.: U. S. Bureau of Prisons, 1971.

875. U. S. Bureau of Prisons. NEW ROLES FOR JAILS: GUIDELINES FOR PLANNING. Washington, D.C.: U. S. Bureau of Prisons, 1969.

876. Abraham, Henry J. THE JUDICIAL PROCESS: AN INTRODUC-
TORY ANALYSIS OF THE COURTS OF THE U.S., ENGLAND
AND FRANCE. New York, N.Y.: Oxford University Press, 1968.

877. Allen, Richard, and others (ed.). READINGS IN LAW AND
PSYCHIATRY. Baltimore, Md.: Johns Hopkins University Press, 1968.

878. American Bar Association. COMPUTERS AND THE LAW. Chicago,
Ill.: American Bar Association, 1969.

879. American Bar Association. THE RIGHTS OF FAIR TRIAL AND
FREE PRESS: AN INFORMATION MANUAL FOR THE BAR, NEWS
MEDIA, LAW ENFORCEMENT OFFICIALS AND COURTS. Chicago,
Ill.: American Bar Association, 1969.

880. American Bar Association. STANDARDS RELATING TO FAIR
TRIAL AND FREE PRESS: APPROVED DRAFT. Chicago, Ill.:
American Bar Association, 1968.

881. American Bar Association. STANDARDS RELATING TO PROVID-
ING DEFENSE SERVICES: APPROVED DRAFT. Chicago, Ill.:
American Bar Association, 1967.

882. American Friends Service Committee. STRUGGLE FOR JUSTICE:
A REPORT ON CRIME AND PUNISHMENT IN AMERICA. New
York, N.Y.: Hill and Wang, 1971.

883. BAIL AND SENTENCING. (Cassette tape, 27 min.) North Hollywood,
Calif.: Center for Cassette Studies.

884. Becker, Theodore L. THE IMPACT OF SUPREME COURT
DECISIONS. New York, N.Y.: Oxford University Press, 1969.

885. Bedau, Hugo. THE DEATH PENALTY IN AMERICA. Chicago, Ill.:
Aldine/Atherton, 1968.

886. Black, Hugo L. A CONSTITUTIONAL FAITH. New York, N.Y.:
Alfred A. Knopf, 1968.

887. Bloomstein, Morris. VERDICT: THE JURY SYSTEM. New York,
N.Y.: Dodd, Mead Co., 1968.

888. Blumberg, Abraham S. (ed.). THE SCALES OF JUSTICE. Chicago, Ill.: Aldine/Atherton, 1970.

889. Byham, William. THE LAW AND PERSONNEL TESTING. Riverside, N.J.: American Management Association, 1971.

890. Carlson, Ronald L. CRIMINAL JUSTICE PROCEDURE FOR POLICE. Buffalo, N.Y.: W. S. Hein and Co., 1970.

★ 891. Casper, Jonathan. AMERICAN CRIMINAL JUSTICE: THE DEFEND-ANT'S PERSPECTIVE. Englewood Cliffs, N.J.: Prentice Hall, 1972.

892. Chambliss, William. CRIME AND LEGAL PROCESS. New York, N.Y.: McGraw-Hill, 1969.

893. Chambliss, William, and Robert Seidman. LAW, ORDER, AND POWER. Reading, Mass.: Addison-Wesley Publishing, 1971.

894. Cicourel, Aaron. THE SOCIAL ORGANIZATION OF JUVENILE JUSTICE. New York, N.Y.: John Wiley and Sons, 1968.

★ 895. Clark, William L. A TREATISE ON THE LAW OF CRIMES. Chicago, Ill.: Callaghan and Co., 1967.

896. Claude, Richard. THE SUPREME COURT AND THE ELECTORAL PROCESS. Baltimore, Md.: Johns Hopkins University Press, 1970.

897. Cohen, Bernard Lande. LAW WITHOUT ORDER: CAPITAL PUNISH-MENT AND THE LIBERALS. New Rochelle, N.Y.: Arlington House, 1970.

898. Colby, Edward. EVERYTHING YOU'VE ALWAYS WANTED TO KNOW ABOUT THE LAW BUT COULDN'T AFFORD TO ASK. New York, N.Y.: Drake, 1972.

899. COUNSEL AND JURISPRUDENCE. (Cassette tape, 27 min.) North Hollywood, Calif.: Center for Cassette Studies.

900. Creamer, J. Shane. A CITIZEN'S GUIDE TO LEGAL RIGHTS. New York, N.Y.: Holt, Rinehart and Winston, 1971.

901. Damgaard, John. STUDENT AND THE COURTS: CAMPUS PRO-FILE. Jericho, N.Y.: Exposition Press, 1971.

902. Dawson, Robert. SENTENCING: THE DECISION AS TO TYPE, LENGTH, AND CONDITIONS OF SENTENCE. Waltham, Mass.: Little, Brown and Co., 1969.

903. Dobrovir, William. JUSTICE IN TIME OF CRISIS. Washington, D.C.: U. S. Government Printing Office, 1969.

★ 904. Downie, Leonard, Jr. JUSTICE DENIED: THE CASE FOR REFORM OF THE COURTS. New York, N.Y.: Praeger Publishers, 1971.

★ 905. Duster, Troy. THE LEGISLATION OF MORALITY: LAW, DRUGS, AND MORAL JUDGMENT. New York, N.Y.: Free Press, 1970.

906. Eisenhower, Milton S. THE RULE OF LAW: AN ALTERNATIVE TO VIOLENCE: A REPORT TO THE NATIONAL COMMISSION ON THE CAUSES AND PREVENTION OF VIOLENCE. North Nashville, Tenn.: Aurora Publishing Co., 1970.

907. Falk, Richard. LEGAL ORDER IN A VIOLENT WORLD. Princeton, N.J.: Princeton University Press, 1968.

908. Frank, John. AMERICAN LAW: THE CASE FOR RADICAL REFORM. Riverside, N.J.: Macmillan Co., 1969.

909. Frankel, Marvin. CRIMINAL SENTENCES: LAW WITHOUT ORDER. New York, N.Y.: Hill and Wang, 1973.

910. Frankel, Sandor. BEYOND A REASONABLE DOUBT. New York, N.Y.: Stein and Day, 1971.

911. Gerber, Rudolph, and Patrick McAnany (eds.). CONTEMPORARY PUNISHMENT: VIEWS, EXPLANATIONS AND JUSTIFICATIONS. Notre Dame, Ind.: University Notre Dame, 1972.

912. Goldstein, Abraham S. THE INSANITY DEFENSE. New Haven, Conn.: Yale University Press, 1967.

913. Grey, David L. THE SUPREME COURT AND THE NEWS MEDIA. Evanston, Ill.: Northwestern University Press, 1968.

★ 914. Hanna, John Paul. TEENAGERS AND THE LAW. Waltham, Mass.: Ginn and Co., 1969.

915. HANDBOOK OF STANDARDS FOR LEGAL AID AND DEFENDER OFFICES. Chicago, Ill.: National Legal Aid and Defender Association, 1970.

★ 916. Hart, Herbert. PUNISHMENT AND RESPONSIBILITY: ESSAYS IN THE PHILOSOPHY OF LAW. New York, N.Y.: Oxford University Press, 1968.

917. Hills, Stuart. CRIME, POWER AND MORALITY: THE CRIMINAL LAW PROCESS IN AMERICA. Scranton, Pa.: Chandler Publishing Co., 1971.

918. Holder, Angela. THE MEANING OF THE CONSTITUTION. Woodbury, N.Y.: Barron Educational Series, 1972.

919. HOW TO ORGANIZE A DEFENDER OFFICE—A HANDBOOK. Chicago, Ill.: National Legal Aid and Defender Association, 1967.

920. Israel, Jerold H. CRIMINAL PROCEDURE IN A NUTSHELL: CONSTITUTIONAL LIMITATIONS. St. Paul, Minn.: West Publishing Co., 1971.

921. Jackson, Percival E. DISSENT AND THE SUPREME COURT: A CHRONOLOGY. Norman, Okla.: University of Oklahoma Press, 1969.

★ 922. James, Howard. CRISIS IN THE COURTS. New York, N.Y.: David McKay Co., 1968.

923. JURIES AND GRAND JURIES. (Cassette tape, 28 min.) North Hollywood, Calif.: Center for Cassette Studies.

924. Kalven, Harry, and Hans Zeisel. THE AMERICAN JURY. Chicago, Ill.: University of Chicago Press, 1971.

925. Karlen, Delmar. JUDICIAL ADMINISTRATION: THE AMERICAN EXPERIENCE. Dobbs Ferry, N.Y.: Oceana Publishing Co., 1970.

★ 926. Kenny, John, and Dan Pursuit. POLICE WORK WITH JUVENILES AND THE ADMINISTRATION OF JUVENILE JUSTICE. Springfield, Ill.: Charles C. Thomas, 1970.

927. Kerbec, Matthew. LEGALLY AVAILABLE U.S. GOVERNMENT INFORMATION AS A RESULT OF THE PUBLIC INFORMATION ACT. Arlington, Va.: Output Systems Corporation, 1970.

928. Klonoski, James, and Robert Mendelsohn. THE POLITICS OF LOCAL JUSTICE. Waltham, Mass.: Little, Brown and Co., 1970.

929. Krislov, Samuel, and others. COMPLIANCE AND THE LAW: A MULTI-DISCIPLINARY APPROACH. Beverly Hills, Calif.: Sage Publishing Co., 1972.

930. LAW AS AUTHORITY. (Cassette tape, 27 min.) North Hollywood, Calif.: Center for Cassette Studies.

931. Leonard, V. A. THE POLICE, THE JUDICIARY, AND THE CRIMINAL. Springfield, Ill.: Charles C. Thomas, 1969.

932. Livingston, Hazel. OFFICER ON THE WITNESS STAND. Los Angeles, Calif.: Legal Book Corporation, 1967.

933. Ludwig, Frederick J. SUPREME COURT DECISIONS AND LAW ENFORCEMENT. Dobbs Ferry, N.Y.: Oceana Publications, 1969.

★ 934. Marshall, James. INTENTION—IN LAW AND SOCIETY. New York, N.Y.: Funk and Wagnalls, 1969.

935. Miller, Frank. CASES AND MATERIALS ON CRIMINAL JUSTICE ADMINISTRATION AND RELATED PROCESSES. Mineola, N.Y.: Foundation Press, 1971.

936. Miller, Frank. THE JUVENILE JUSTICE PROCESS. Mineola, N.Y.: Foundation Press, 1971.

937. Milner, Neal. THE COURT AND LOCAL LAW ENFORCEMENT: THE IMPACT OF MIRANDA. Beverly Hills, Calif.: Sage Publications, 1971.

938. Mitchell, Roger S. THE HOMOSEXUAL AND THE LAW. New York, N.Y.: Arco Publishing Co., 1969.

939. Mueller, Gerhard O. COMPARATIVE CRIMINAL PROCEDURE. New York, N.Y.: New York University Press, 1969.

940. National Council on Crime and Delinquency. MODEL RULES OF COURT ON POLICE ACTION FROM ARREST TO ARRAIGNMENT. New York, N.Y.: National Council on Crime and Delinquency, 1969.

★ 941. Nedrud, Duane R. THE SUPREME COURT AND THE LAW OF CRIMINAL INVESTIGATION. Chicago, Ill.: L. E. Publishers, 1969.

942. Nilsson, F., and R. Bullock. STUDYING CRIMINAL COURT PROCESSES—SOME TOOLS AND TECHNIQUES. Springfield, Va.: National Technical Information Service, 1970.

943. Norwick, Kenneth (ed.). YOUR LEGAL RIGHTS: MAKING THE LAW WORK FOR YOU. New York, N.Y.: John Day, 1972.

944. Pantaleoni, C. A. HANDBOOK OF COURTROOM DEMEANOR AND TESTIMONY. Englewood Cliffs, N.J.: Prentice Hall, 1971.

945. Pound, Roscoe. SOCIAL CONTROL THROUGH LAW. Hamden, Conn.: Shoe String Press, 1968.

946. Prince, Jerome. CASES AND MATERIALS ON EVIDENCE. Mineola, N.Y.: Foundation Press, 1972.

947. Radzinowicz, Leon, and Marvin Wolfgang. CRIME AND JUSTICE. (3 vols.) Scranton, Pa.: Basic Books, 1971.

948. Rosenblatt, Stanley. JUSTICE DENIED. Los Angeles, Calif.: Nash Publishing Corporation, 1971.

949. Rothstein, Paul. EVIDENCE IN A NUTSHELL. St. Paul, Minn.: West Publishing Co., 1970.

950. Schafer, William J. CONFESSIONS AND STATEMENTS. Springfield, Ill.: Charles C. Thomas, 1968.

951. Schubert, Glendon. JUDICIAL POLICY-MAKING. Oakland, N.J.: Scott Foresman and Co., 1968.

952. Schwartz, Richard, and Jerome Skolnick. SOCIETY AND THE LEGAL ORDER. Scranton, Pa.: Basic Books, 1970.

953. Shapiro, Martin M. (ed.). THE SUPREME COURT AND PUBLIC POLICY. Oakland, N.J.: Scott Foresman and Co., 1969.

★ 954. Sigler, Jay A. AN INTRODUCTION TO THE LEGAL SYSTEM. Homewood, Ill.: Dorsey Press, 1968.

955. Simon, Rita. THE JURY AND THE DEFENSE OF INSANITY. Waltham, Mass.: Little, Brown and Co., 1967.

956. Smith, Edgar. BRIEF AGAINST DEATH. New York, N.Y.: Alfred A. Knopf, 1968.

957. Smith, G. W. STATISTICAL ANALYSIS OF PUBLIC DEFENDER ACTIVITIES. Springfield, Va.: National Technical Information Service, 1970.

958. Sobel, Nathan. EYE-WITNESS IDENTIFICATION: LEGAL AND PRACTICAL PROBLEMS. New York, N.Y.: C. Boardman, 1972.

959. Stuckey, Gilbert B. EVIDENCE FOR THE LAW ENFORCEMENT OFFICER. New York, N.Y.: McGraw-Hill, 1968.

960. Sussmann, Frederick B., and F. S. Baum. LAW OF JUVENILE DELINQUENCY. Dobbs Ferry, N.Y.: Oceana Publishing Co., 1968.

961. Sykes, Gresham M. LAW AND THE LAWLESS: A READER IN CRIMINOLOGY. Westminster, Md.: Random House, 1969.

962. TAKING THE FIFTH! (Cassette tape, 29 min.) North Hollywood, Calif.: Center for Cassette Studies.

963. TESTIFYING IN COURT. (Sound filmstrip, color.) Gaithersburg, Md.: International Association of Chiefs of Police.

★ 964. Tierney, Kevin. COURTROOM TESTIMONY: A POLICEMAN'S GUIDE. New York, N.Y.: Funk and Wagnalls, 1970.

965. Ulmer, S. Disney. MILITARY JUSTICE AND THE RIGHT TO COUNSEL. Lexington, Ky.: University Press of Kentucky, 1970.

966. U. S. Committee on the Judiciary. TO ABOLISH THE DEATH PENALTY: HEARINGS...BEFORE...90th CONGRESS, 2nd SESSION...MARCH 20, 21, AND JULY 2, 1968. Washington, D.C.: U. S. Government Printing Office, 1970.

967. U. S. Congress (Senate). THE CRIMINAL JUSTICE ACT IN THE FEDERAL DISTRICT COURTS. Washington, D.C.: U. S. Government Printing Office, 1969.

968. U. S. Law Enforcement Assistance Administration. JUSTICE IN THE STATES. (Addresses and Papers of the National Conference on the Judiciary.) Washington, D.C.: U. S. Department of Justice, 1971.

969. U. S. Law Enforcement Assistance Administration. PLANNING AND DESIGNING FOR JUVENILE JUSTICE. Washington, D.C.: U. S. Department of Justice, 1972.

970. U. S. Law Enforcement Assistance Administration. REHABILITA- TIVE PLANNING SERVICES FOR THE CRIMINAL DEFENSE. Washington, D.C.: U. S. Government Printing Office, 1970.

★ 971. U. S. National Commission on Prevention of Violence. LAW AND ORDER RECONSIDERED. Washington, D.C.: U. S. Government Printing Office, 1969.

972. Van Allen, Edward J. OUR HANDCUFFED POLICE. Mineola, N.Y.: Reportorial Press, 1968.

973. Wasserstein, Bruce, and Mark Green. WITH JUSTICE FOR SOME: AN INDICTMENT OF THE LAW BY YOUNG ADVOCATES. Boston, Mass.: Beacon Press, 1972.

★ 974. Weston, Paul B., and Kenneth Wells. THE ADMINISTRATION OF JUSTICE. Englewood Cliffs, N.J.: Prentice Hall, 1973.

★ 975. Weston, Paul, and Kenneth Wells. FUNDAMENTALS OF EVIDENCE. Englewood Cliffs, N.J.: Prentice Hall, 1972.

976. White, William. WINNING IN COURT ON THE LAW OF FACTS. Englewood Cliffs, N.J.: Prentice Hall, 1972.

★ 977. Wright, G. R., and J. Marlo. POLICE OFFICER AND CRIMINAL JUSTICE. New York, N.Y.: McGraw-Hill, 1970.

JUVENILE COURT

See also Behavioral and Social Science
Civil Rights
Community Based Corrections:
    Adult/Juvenile
Correctional Institutions:
    Adult/Juvenile

Juvenile Delinquency
Probation and Parole:
    Adult/Juvenile
Student Disorders

★ 978. Emerson, Robert M. JUDGING DELINQUENTS: CONTEXT AND PROCESS IN JUVENILE COURTS. Chicago, Ill.: Aldine/Atherton, 1969.

979. George, B. James, Jr. GAULT AND THE JUVENILE COURT REVOLUTION. Ann Arbor, Mich.: Institute of Continuing Legal Education, 1968.

980. Joint Commission on Corrections, Manpower and Training. THE FUTURE OF THE JUVENILE COURT: IMPLICATIONS FOR CORRECTIONAL MANPOWER AND TRAINING. Washington, D.C.: American Correctional Association, 1968.

981. Ketcham, Orman W., and Monrad G. Paulsen. CASES AND MATERIALS RELATING TO JUVENILE COURTS. Mineola, N.Y.: Foundation Press, 1967.

★ 982. Lemert, Edwin M. SOCIAL ACTION AND LEGAL CHANGE: REVOLUTION WITHIN THE JUVENILE COURT. Chicago, Ill.: Aldine/Atherton, 1970.

983. Lou, Herbert. JUVENILE COURTS IN THE UNITED STATES. New York, N.Y.: Arno Press, 1972.

984. National Council on Crime and Delinquency. MODEL RULES FOR JUVENILE COURTS. New York, N.Y.: National Council on Crime and Delinquency, 1969.

985. St. Louis University. THE JUVENILE COURT: DIRECTIONS FOR THE FUTURE. St. Louis, Mo.: St. Louis University Press, 1967.

986. Sloan, Irving J. YOUTH AND THE LAW: RIGHTS, PRIVILEGES AND OBLIGATIONS. Dobbs Ferry, N.Y.: Oceana Publishing Co., 1970.

987. U. S. Center for Studies in Crime and Delinquency. National Institute of Mental Health. INSTEAD OF COURT—DIVERSION IN JUVENILE JUSTICE. Washington, D.C.: U. S. Government Printing Office, 1971.

★ 988. U. S. Center for Studies in Crime and Delinquency. National Institute of Mental Health. THE JUVENILE COURT: A STATUS REPORT. Washington, D.C.: U. S. Government Printing Office, 1971.

JUVENILE DELINQUENCY

See also Behavioral and Social Science
Classification of: Crime/Offenders
Criminology
Domestic Relations

Drug: Information/
   Treatment
Student Disorders
Support Services

989. Ahlstrom, Winton, and Robert Havighurst. FOUR HUNDRED LOSERS: DELINQUENT BOYS IN HIGH SCHOOL. San Francisco, Calif.: Jossey-Bass, 1971.

990. Amos, William E., and Charles F. Wellford. DELINQUENCY PREVENTION: THEORY AND PRACTICE. Englewood Cliffs, N.J.: Prentice Hall, 1967.

991. Bacon, Margaret, and Mary B. Jones. TEEN-AGE DRINKING. New York, N.Y.: Thomas Crowell Co., 1968.

992. Bersani, Carl A. (ed.). CRIME AND DELINQUENCY: A READER. Riverside, N.J.: Macmillan Co., 1970.

★ 993. Cain, Arthur H. YOUNG PEOPLE AND CRIME. New York, N.Y.: John Day, 1968.

994. Caldwell, Robert, and James Black. JUVENILE DELINQUENCY. New York, N.Y.: Ronald Press Co., 1971.

995. Carpenter, Mary. JUVENILE DELINQUENTS: THEIR CONDITION AND TREATMENT. Montclair, N.J.: Patterson-Smith, 1970.

996. Cederbaums, Juris. THE LEGAL NORMS OF DELINQUENCY: A COMPARATIVE STUDY. Hackensack, N.J.: Fred B. Rothman, 1969.

997. Cortes, Juan, and Florence Gatti. DELINQUENCY AND CRIME, A BIOPHYSICAL APPROACH: EMPIRICAL, THEORETICAL AND PRACTICAL ASPECTS OF CRIMINAL BEHAVIOR. New York, N.Y.: Seminar Press, 1972.

998. Cressey, Donald R., and David A. Ward. DELINQUENCY, CRIME AND SOCIAL PROCESS. New York, N.Y.: Harper and Row, 1969.

999. Eisner, Victor. THE DELINQUENCY LABEL: THE EPIDEMIOLOGY OF JUVENILE DELINQUENCY. Westminster, Md.: Random House, 1969.

★1000. Eldefonso, Edward. LAW ENFORCEMENT AND THE YOUTHFUL OFFENDERS: JUVENILE PROCEDURES. New York, N.Y.: John Wiley and Sons, 1972.

1001. Empey, Lamar. THE SILVERLAKE EXPERIMENT TESTING DELINQUENCY THEORY AND COMMUNITY INTERVENTION. Chicago, Ill.: Aldine/Atherton, 1971.

★1002. Empey, Lamar, and Steven Lubeck. DELINQUENCY PREVENTION STRATEGIES. Washington, D.C.: U. S. Government Printing Office, 1970.

1003. Garabedian, Peter, and Don Gibbons. BECOMING DELINQUENT: YOUNG OFFENDERS AND THE CORRECTIONAL PROCESS. Chicago, Ill.: Aldine/Atherton, 1970.

1004. Gibbons, Don C. DELINQUENT BEHAVIOR. Englewood Cliffs, N.J.: Prentice Hall, 1970.

1005. Glueck, Sheldon. PREDICTING DELINQUENCY AND CRIME. Cambridge, Mass.: Harvard University Press, 1967.

1006. Hahn, Paul. THE JUVENILE OFFENDER AND THE LAW. Cincinnati, Ohio: W. H. Anderson Co., 1971.

1007. Halloran, James Dermont. MASS MEDIA AND DELINQUENT BEHAVIOR. New York, N.Y.: Humanities Press, 1970.

1008. Halloran, J. D., and others. TELEVISION AND DELINQUENCY. New York, N.Y.: Humanities Press, 1970.

1009. Hanna, John Paul. TEENAGERS AND THE LAW. Boston, Mass.: Ginn and Co., 1967.

1010. Haskell, Martin, and Lewis Yablonsky. CRIME AND DELINQUENCY. Chicago, Ill.: Rand McNally, 1970.

1011. Hirschi, Travis. CAUSES OF DELINQUENCY. Berkeley, Calif.: University of California Press, 1969.

★1012. Hirschi, Travis, and Hanan C. Servin. DELINQUENCY RESEARCH. New York, N.Y.: Free Press, 1967.

1013. Hopson, Dan, and others. THE JUVENILE OFFENDER AND THE LAW: A SYMPOSIUM. New York, N.Y.: DeCapo Press, 1968.

1014. JUVENILE DELINQUENCY. (Sound filmstrip, color.) Gaithersburg, Md.: International Association of Chiefs of Police.

★1015. Kenney, John P. POLICE WORK WITH JUVENILES AND THE ADMINISTRATION OF JUVENILE JUSTICE. Springfield, Ill.: Charles C. Thomas, 1970.

★1016. Klein, Malcolm W., and Barbara G. Myerhoff (eds.). JUVENILE GANGS IN CONTEXT: THEORY, RESEARCH AND ACTION. Englewood Cliffs, N.J.: Prentice Hall, 1967.

1017. Kobetz, Richard W. THE POLICE ROLE AND JUVENILE DELIN-QUENCY. Gaithersburg, Md.: International Association of Chiefs of Police, 1971.

1018. Korn, Richard R. (ed.). JUVENILE DELINQUENCY. New York, N.Y.: Thomas Y. Crowell, 1968.

1019. Leinwand, Gerald. CRIME AND JUVENILE DELINQUENCY: PROBLEMS OF AMERICAN SOCIETY. New York, N.Y.: Washington Square Press, 1968.

1020. Lerman, Paul. DELINQUENCY AND SOCIAL POLICY. New York, N.Y.: Praeger Publishers, 1970.

★1021. Lobel, Lester H., and M. Wylie. DELINQUENCY CAN BE STOPPED. New York, N.Y.: McGraw-Hill, 1967.

1022. McDonald, Lynn. SOCIAL CLASS AND DELINQUENCY. Hamden, Conn.: Archon Books, 1969.

★1023. Martin, John, and others. THE ANALYSIS OF DELINQUENT BEHAVIOR: A STRUCTURAL APPROACH. Westminster, Md.: Random House, 1970.

1024. Martin, J. M., and J. P. Fitzpatrick. ANALYZING DELINQUENT BEHAVIOR—A NEW APPROACH. Washington, D.C.: U.S. Government Printing Office, 1968.

1025. Morris, Joe Alex. FIRST OFFENDER: A VOLUNTEER PROGRAM FOR YOUTH IN TROUBLE WITH THE LAW. New York, N.Y.: Funk and Wagnalls, 1970.

1026. Mueller, Gerhard, and others. DELINQUENCY AND PUBERTY EXAMINATION OF A JUVENILE: DELINQUENCY FAD. Hackensack, N.J.: Fred B. Rothman, 1971.

1027. Norman, Sherwood. DELINQUENCY PREVENTION: THREE BASIC APPROACHES. Dobbs Ferry, N.Y.: Oceana Publications, 1968.

1028. Norman, Sherwood. THE YOUTH SERVICE BUREAU: A KEY TO DELINQUENCY PREVENTION. Paramas, N.J.: National Council on Crime and Delinquency, 1972.

1029. Platt, Anthony M. THE CHILD SAVERS: THE INVENTION OF DELINQUENCY. Chicago, Ill.: University of Chicago Press, 1969.

*1030. President's Commission on Law Enforcement and Administration of Justice. JUVENILE DELINQUENCY AND YOUTH CRIME: TASK FORCE REPORT. Washington, D.C.: U.S. Government Printing Office, 1967.

1031. President's Council on Youth Opportunity. MANUAL FOR YOUTH COORDINATORS. Washington, D.C.: U.S. Government Printing Office, 1969.

1032. Robison, Sophia. JUVENILE DELINQUENCY: ITS NATURE AND CONTROL. New York, N.Y.: Holt, Rinehart and Winston, 1969.

1033. Roff, M. SERVICE-RELATED EXPERIENCE OF A SAMPLE OF JUVENILE DELINQUENTS AND THE RELATION BETWEEN EDUCATION, NUMBER OF JUVENILE APPREHENSIONS, AND OUTCOME IN SERVICE. Springfield, Va.: National Technical Information Service, 1968.

1034. Rosenberg, Bernard. THE VARIETIES OF DELINQUENT EXPERIENCE. Waltham, Mass.: Blaisdell Publishing Co., 1969.

*1035. Rosenquist, Carl M., and Edwin Megargee. DELINQUENCY IN THREE CULTURES. Austin, Tex.: University of Texas Press, 1969.

1036. Roucek, Joseph Slabey. JUVENILE DELINQUENCY. Freeport, N.Y.: Books for Libraries, 1970.

*1037. Schafer, Stephen, and Richard Knudten. JUVENILE DELINQUENCY: AN INTRODUCTION. Westminster, Md.: Random House, 1970.

1038. Short, James. GANG DELINQUENCY AND DELINQUENT SUBCULTURES. New York, N.Y.: Harper and Row, 1971.

*1039. Spergel, Irving A. COMMUNITY PROBLEM SOLVING: THE DELINQUENCY EXAMPLE. Chicago, Ill.: University of Chicago Press, 1969.

1040. Steel, Ronald. NEW LIGHT ON JUVENILE DELINQUENCY. New York, N.Y.: H. W. Wilson Co., 1967.

★1041. Stratton, John R., and Robert M. Terry (eds.). PREVENTION OF
        DELINQUENCY: PROBLEMS AND PROGRAMS. Riverside, N.J.:
        Macmillan Co., 1968.

 1042. Tomaino, Louis. CHANGING THE DELINQUENT—A PRACTICAL
        APPROACH. Austin, Tex.: Hogg Foundation of Mental Health,
        1969.

 1043. U. S. Office of Juvenile Delinquency and Youth Development. ALTER-
        NATIVES TO INCARCERATION. Washington, D.C.: U. S. Government
        Printing Office, 1967.

 1044. U. S. Office of Juvenile Delinquency and Youth Development. ANALYZ-
        ING DELINQUENT BEHAVIOR: A NEW APPROACH. Washington,
        D.C.: U. S. Government Printing Office, 1968.

 1045. U. S. Office of Juvenile Delinquency and Youth Development. WHY
        CHILDREN ARE IN JAIL AND HOW TO KEEP THEM OUT.
        Washington, D.C.: U. S. Office of Juvenile Delinquency and Youth
        Development, 1970.

 1046. U. S. Youth Development and Delinquency Prevention Administration.
        DELINQUENCY PREVENTION STRATEGIES. Washington, D.C.:
        U. S. Government Printing Office, 1970.

 1047. U. S. Youth Development and Delinquency Prevention Administration.
        DELINQUENCY TODAY: A GUIDE FOR COMMUNITY ACTION.
        Washington, D.C.: U. S. Government Printing Office, 1971.

 1048. U. S. Youth Development and Delinquency Prevention Administration.
        JUVENILE DELINQUENCY PLANNING. Washington, D.C.: U. S.
        Government Printing Office, 1971.

 1049. U. S. Youth Development and Delinquency Prevention Administration.
        TOWARD A POLITICAL DEFINITION OF JUVENILE DELIN-
        QUENCY. Washington, D.C.: U. S. Government Printing Office, 1970.

 1050. Vedder, Clyde B. JUVENILE OFFENDERS. Springfield, Ill.: Charles
        C. Thomas, 1971.

 1051. Vedder, Clyde, and Dora Somerville. THE DELINQUENT GIRL.
        Springfield, Ill.: Charles C. Thomas, 1970.

★1052. West, D. J. THE YOUNG OFFENDER. New York, N.Y.: International
        Universities Press, 1967.

★1053. Wheeler, Stanton. CONTROLLING DELINQUENTS. New York,
        N.Y.: John Wiley and Sons, 1968.

1054.   THE YOUNG OFFENDER. (Cassette tape, 28 min.) North Hollywood, Calif.: Center for Cassette Studies.

LAWS AND STATUTES

See also **Behavioral and Social Science   Judicial Process**
         Civil Rights   Juvenile Court
         Court: Management and   Prosecution
             Operations/Structure

1055.   American Bar Association. FIREARMS AND LEGISLATIVE REGU-LATION. Chicago, Ill.: American Bar Association, 1967.

1056.   Ashman, Allan. LAWS OF ARREST, SEARCH, SEIZURE, AND EVIDENCE. Chapel Hill, N.C.: University of North Carolina, Institute of Government, 1967.

1057.   Bassiouni, M. Cherif. CRIMINAL LAW AND ITS PROCESSES: THE LAW OF PUBLIC ORDER. Springfield, Ill.: Charles C. Thomas, 1969.

1058.   Bedau, Hugo Adam. THE DEATH PENALTY IN AMERICA. Chicago, Ill.: Aldine/Atherton, 1968.

1059.   Black, Charles L. STRUCTURE AND RELATIONSHIP IN CON-STITUTIONAL LAW. Baton Rouge, La.: Louisiana State University Press, 1969.

1060.   Calvert, Eric Roy. CAPITAL PUNISHMENT IN THE TWENTIETH CENTURY. Port Washington, N.Y.: Kennikat, 1971.

★1061.   Chamelin, Neil, and Kenneth Evans. CRIMINAL LAW FOR POLICE-MEN. Englewood Cliffs, N.J.: Prentice Hall, 1971.

1062.   Chamelin, Neil, and Kenneth Evans. HANDBOOK OF CRIMINAL LAW. Englewood Cliffs, N.J.: Prentice Hall, 1972.

1063.   Creamer, J. Shane. THE LAW OF ARREST, SEARCH & SEIZURE. Philadelphia, Pa.: W. B. Saunders Co., 1968.

1064.   Garnfield, David. THE ABORTION DECISION. Garden City, N.Y.: Doubleday and Co., 1969.

★1065.   Heathcock, Claude. THE UNITED STATES CONSTITUTION IN PERSPECTIVE. Boston, Mass.: Allyn, 1972.

1066.   Inbau, Fred. CRIMINAL LAW FOR THE POLICE. Philadelphia, Pa.: Chilton Book Co., 1969.

1067. Inbau, Fred, and Marvin Aspen. CRIMINAL LAW FOR THE LAYMAN: A GUIDE FOR CITIZEN AND STUDENT. Philadelphia, Pa.: Chilton Book Co., 1970.

1068. Kadish, Sanford, and Monrad G. Paulsen. CRIMINAL LAW AND ITS PROCESSES: CASES AND MATERIALS. Waltham, Mass.: Little, Brown and Co., 1969.

★1069. Klotter, John C. CONSTITUTIONAL LAW FOR POLICE. Cincinnati, Ohio: W. H. Anderson, 1968.

1070. LEGISLATIVE HISTORY OF THE 1971 AMENDMENT TO THE OMNIBUS CRIME CONTROL AND SAFE STREETS ACT OF 1968. Washington, D.C.: U. S. Government Printing Office, 1972.

1071. Levy, Leonard W. ORIGINS OF THE FIFTH AMENDMENT: THE RIGHT AGAINST SELF-INCRIMINATION. New York, N.Y.: Oxford University Press, 1968.

1072. Lockhart, William, and others. CONSTITUTIONAL LAW: CASES, COMMENTS, QUESTIONS. St. Paul, Minn.: West Publishing Co., 1967.

1073. Lockhart, William, and others. THE AMERICAN CONSTITUTION: CASES AND MATERIALS. St. Paul, Minn.: West Publishing Co., 1967.

★1074. Mason, Alpheus, and William Beaney. AMERICAN CONSTITU-TIONAL LAW: INTRODUCTORY ESSAYS AND CONSTITUTIONAL LAW. Englewood Cliffs, N.J.: Prentice Hall, 1972.

1075. National Commission on the Reform of Federal Criminal Law. FINAL REPORT—PROPOSED NEW FEDERAL CRIMINAL CODE (TITLE 18, U. S. CODE). Washington, D.C.: U. S. Government Printing Office, 1971.

★1076. Perkins, Rollin M. CRIMINAL LAW. Mineola, N.Y.: Foundation Press, 1969.

★1077. Schwartz, Bernard. CONSTITUTIONAL LAW: A TEXTBOOK. Riverside, N.J.: Macmillan Co., 1972.

1078. Shoolbred, Claude. A GUIDE TO RECENT CRIMINAL LEGISLA-TION. Elmsford, N.Y.: Pergamon Press, 1968.

1079. Taylor, Telford. TWO STUDIES IN CONSTITUTIONAL INTERPRE-TATIONS. Columbus, Ohio: Ohio State University Press, 1969.

★1080. Tresolini, Roco J. AMERICAN CONSTITUTIONAL LAW. Riverside, N.J.: Macmillan Co., 1970.

1081. U. S. Laws. PUBLIC LAW 91-452 ORGANIZED CRIME CONTROL ACT OF 1970. Washington, D.C.: U. S. Government Printing Office, 1970.

1082. U. S. National Advisory Commission on Civil Disorder. SUPPLEMENTAL STUDIES FOR THE NATIONAL ADVISORY COMMISSION ON CIVIL DISORDERS. Washington, D.C.: U. S. Government Printing Office, 1968.

1083. Weinreb, Lloyd L. CRIMINAL LAW: CASES, COMMENTS, QUESTIONS. Mineola, N.Y.: Foundation Press, 1969.

★1084. Young, Rudolph. CRIMINAL LAW: CODES AND CASES. New York, N.Y.: McGraw-Hill, 1972.

ORGANIZED CRIME

See also **Behavioral and Social Science**   **Judicial Process**
Classification of: Crime/Offenders   **Laws and Statutes**
Crime Deterrence and Prevention   **Victimless Crime**
Criminology

1085. Chamber of Commerce of the U. S. DESKBOOK ON ORGANIZED CRIME. Washington, D.C.: Chamber of Commerce of the U. S., 1969.

★1086. Cressey, Donald. THEFT OF THE NATION: THE STRUCTURE AND OPERATIONS OF ORGANIZED CRIME IN AMERICA. New York, N.Y.: Harper and Row, 1969.

1087. Gardiner, J. A. POLITICS OF CORRUPTION: ORGANIZED CRIME IN AN AMERICAN CITY. New York, N.Y.: Russell Sage Foundation, 1970.

1088. Gartner, Michael. CRIME AND BUSINESS: WHAT YOU SHOULD KNOW ABOUT THE INFILTRATION OF CRIME INTO BUSINESS AND OF BUSINESS INTO CRIME. Princeton, N.J.: Dow Jones, 1971.

1089. Hutchinson, John. IMPERFECT UNION: CORRUPTION IN AMERICAN TRADE UNIONS. New York, N.Y.: E. P. Dutton and Co., 1972.

1090. Ianni, Francis. A FAMILY BUSINESS: KINSHIP AND SOCIAL CONTROL IN ORGANIZED CRIME. New York, N.Y.: Russell Sage Foundation, 1972.

1091. King, Rufus. GAMBLING AND ORGANIZED CRIME. Washington, D.C.: Public Affairs Press, 1969.

1092. Maas, Peter. THE VALACHI PAPERS. New York, N.Y.: G. P. Putnam, 1968.

1093. Moscow, Alvin. MERCHANTS OF HEROIN. New York, N.Y.: Dial Press Co., 1968.

1094. President's Commission on Law Enforcement and Administration of Justice. ORGANIZED CRIME: TASK FORCE REPORT. Washington, D.C.: U. S. Government Printing Office, 1967.

1095. Reid, Ed. THE GRIM REAPERS: THE ANATOMY OF ORGANIZED CRIME IN AMERICA. Chicago, Ill.: Henry Regnery Co., 1969.

1096. Salerno, Ralph, and John S. Tompkins. THE CRIME CONFEDERA-TION: COSA NOSTRA AND ALLIED OPERATIONS IN ORGANIZED CRIME. Garden City, N.Y.: Doubleday and Co., 1969.

1097. U. S. Committee on Government Operations. FEDERAL EFFORT AGAINST ORGANIZED CRIME: REPORT OF AGENCY OPERA-TIONS. Washington, D.C.: U. S. Government Printing Office, 1968.

1098. U. S. Committee on Government Operations. FEDERAL EFFORT AGAINST ORGANIZED CRIME: ROLE OF THE PRIVATE SECTOR. Washington, D.C.: U. S. Government Printing Office, 1971.

1099. U. S. Law Enforcement Assistance Administration. ORGANIZED CRIME: THE NEED FOR RESEARCH. Washington, D.C.: U. S. Law Enforcement Assistance Administration, 1970.

1100. U. S. Law Enforcement Assistance Administration. THE PENETRA-TION OF LEGITIMATE BUSINESS BY ORGANIZED CRIME: AN ANALYSIS. Washington, D.C.: U. S. Law Enforcement Assistance Administration, 1970.

★1101. U. S. Law Enforcement Assistance Administration. POLICE GUIDE ON ORGANIZED CRIME. Washington, D.C.: U. S. Law Enforcement Assistance Administration, 1972.

PERSONNEL ADMINISTRATION

See also **Communications: Data/Visual/**   **Police Organization**
     Voice/Equipment   **Police Patrol Function**
   Education   **Police Traffic Function**
   Information: Systems/Software   **Security Systems**
   Planning and Evaluation   **Support Services**
   Police Internal Affairs   **Training**
   Police Management

★1102. Alex, Nicholas. BLACK IN BLUE: A STUDY OF THE NEGRO POLICEMAN. New York, N.Y.: Appleton-Century-Crofts, 1969.

1103. American Bar Association. Advisory Committee on the Police Function. STANDARDS RELATING TO THE URBAN POLICE FUNCTION (TENTATIVE DRAFT). Chicago, Ill.: American Bar Association, 1972.

1104. Anastasi, Anne. PSYCHOLOGICAL TESTING. Riverside, N.J.: Macmillan Co., 1968.

1105. Arco Editorial Board. LIEUTENANT, POLICE DEPARTMENT. New York, N.Y.: Arco Publishing Co., 1969.

1106. Arco Editorial Board. PATROLMAN, POLICE DEPARTMENT. New York, N.Y.: Arco Publishing Co., 1969.

1107. Arco Editorial Board. POLICEWOMAN. New York, N.Y.: Arco Publishing Co., 1970.

1108. Arco Editorial Board. SERGEANT, POLICE DEPARTMENT. New York, N.Y.: Arco Publishing Co., 1968.

1109. Argyris, Chris. PERSONALITY AND ORGANIZATION. New York, N.Y.: Harper and Row, 1970.

★1110. Arm, Walter. THE POLICEMAN: AN INSIDE LOOK AT HIS ROLE IN MODERN SOCIETY. New York, N.Y.: Dutton Publishing Co., 1969.

1111. Aussieker, M. W. POLICE COLLECTIVE BARGAINING. Chicago, Ill.: Public Personnel Association, 1969.

1112. Baer, Walter E. GRIEVANCE HANDLING: 101 GUIDES FOR SUPERVISORS. Riverside, N.J.: American Management Association, 1970.

1113. Berenson, Conrad. JOB DESCRIPTIONS: HOW TO WRITE AND USE THEM. Swarthmore, Pa.: Arthur Croft, 1968.

1114. Berkley, George E. THE DEMOCRATIC POLICEMAN. Boston, Mass.: Beacon Press, 1969.

1115. Biegeleisen, J. I. JOB RESUMES: HOW TO WRITE THEM, HOW TO PRESENT THEM. New York, N.Y.: Grosset and Dunlap, 1969.

1116. Bittel, Lester R. WHAT EVERY SUPERVISOR SHOULD KNOW. New York, N.Y.: McGraw-Hill, 1968.

★1117. Bittner, Egon. THE FUNCTIONS OF THE POLICE IN MODERN SOCIETY. Washington, D.C.: U. S. Government Printing Office, 1970.

1118. Boettinger, Henry M. MOVING MOUNTAINS OR THE ART AND CRAFT OF LETTING OTHERS SEE THINGS YOUR WAY. Riverside, N.J.: Macmillan Co., 1969.

★1119. Bopp, William J. THE POLICE REBELLION: A QUEST FOR BLUE POWER. Springfield, Ill.: Charles C. Thomas, 1971.

★1120. Bristow, Allen P. EFFECTIVE POLICE MANPOWER UTILIZATION. Springfield, Ill.: Charles C. Thomas, 1969.

1121. Bristow, Allen P. (ed.). POLICE SUPERVISION READINGS. Springfield, Ill.: Charles C. Thomas, 1970.

1122. Burby, Raymond J. COMMUNICATING WITH PEOPLE: THE SUPERVISOR'S INTRODUCTION TO VERBAL COMMUNICATION AND DECISIONMAKING. Reading, Mass.: Addison-Wesley Publishing Co., 1970.

1123. Collett, Merrill, and others. STREAMLINING PERSONNEL COMMUNICATIONS. Chicago, Ill.: Public Personnel Association, 1969.

1124. Cowles Book Company, Inc. PRACTICE FOR CIVIL SERVICE POLICE DEPARTMENT PROMOTION EXAMINATION. Chicago, Ill.: Cowles Book Co., 1969.

1125. Cribbin, James. EFFECTIVE MANAGERIAL LEADERSHIP. Riverside, N.J.: American Management Association, 1972.

1126. Donovan, J. J. RECRUITMENT AND SELECTION IN THE PUBLIC SERVICE. Chicago, Ill.: Public Personnel Association, 1968.

1127. Dowling, William F. HOW MANAGERS MOTIVATE: THE IMPERATIVES OF SUPERVISION. New York, N.Y.: McGraw-Hill, 1971.

1128. Educational Testing Service. PROCEDURES USED IN NEW YORK CITY FOR PROMOTING POLICE OFFICERS TO SERGEANT, LIEUTENANT, AND CAPTAIN: SURVEY AND RECOMMENDATIONS. Princeton, N.J.: Educational Testing Service, 1970.

1129. Famularo, Joseph (ed.). HANDBOOK OF MODERN PERSONNEL ADMINISTRATION. New York, N.Y.: McGraw-Hill, 1972.

1130. Fiedler, Fred E. A THEORY OF LEADERSHIP EFFECTIVENESS. New York, N.Y.: McGraw-Hill, 1967.

1131. Furcon, John. SOME QUESTIONS AND ANSWERS ABOUT POLICE OFFICER SELECTION TESTING. Occasional Papers Series No. 35. Chicago, Ill.: Industrial Relations Center, University of Chicago, 1972.

1132. Gellerman, Saul W. MANAGEMENT BY MOTIVATION. Riverside, N.J.: American Management Association, 1968.

1133. Gofke, Blye, and Stallings. POLICE SERGEANTS MANUAL. Los Angeles, Calif.: Legal Book Corporation, 1972.

1134. Haimann, Theo, and Raymond Hilgert. SUPERVISION: CONCEPTS AND PRACTICES OF MANAGEMENT. Cincinnati, Ohio: South-Western Publishing Co., 1972.

★1135. Hansen, David, and Thomas Culley. THE POLICE LEADER: A HAND-BOOK. Springfield, Ill.: Charles C. Thomas, 1971.

1136. Hariton, Theodore. INTERVIEW: THE EXECUTIVE'S GUIDE TO SELECTING THE RIGHT PERSONNEL. New York, N.Y.: Hastings House Publishing, 1970.

1137. Hawk, Roger H. THE RECRUITMENT FUNCTION. Riverside, N.J.: American Management Association, 1967.

1138. HOW TO BE SUPERVISED. (Sound filmstrip, color.) Gaithersburg, Md.: International Association of Chiefs of Police.

★1139. Iannone, N. F., and James Stinchcomb. SUPERVISION OF POLICE PERSONNEL. Englewood Cliffs, N.J.: Prentice Hall, 1970.

1140. International Association of Chiefs of Police. POLICE PERSONNEL SELECTION SURVEY. Gaithersburg, Md.: International Association of Chiefs of Police, 1968.

1141. Keefe, William F. LISTEN, MANAGEMENT. New York, N.Y.: McGraw-Hill, 1971.

1142. Kirkpatrick, James J., and others. TESTING AND FAIR EMPLOY-MENT: FAIRNESS AND VALIDITY OF PERSONNEL TESTS FOR DIFFERENT ETHNIC GROUPS. New York, N.Y.: New York University Press, 1968.

1143. Koch, Harry. FACTS AND STRATEGY FOR POLICE PROMO-TIONAL EXAMINATIONS. San Francisco, Calif.: Ken-Books, 1967.

★1144. Leonard, V. A. POLICE PERSONNEL ADMINISTRATION. Springfield, Ill.: Charles C. Thomas, 1970.

1145. Meares, Ainslie. HOW TO BE A BOSS: A PRACTICING PSYCHIA-TRIST OF THE MANAGING OF MEN. New York, N.Y.: Coward, McCann and Goeghagen, 1971.

★1146. Melnicoe, William B., and Jan Mennig. ELEMENTS OF POLICE SUPERVISION. Riverside, N.J.: Glencoe Press, 1969.

1147. Miles, John, and others. LAW OFFICER'S POCKET MANUAL. Los Angeles, Calif.: Bureau of International Affairs, 1972.

1148. Miller, Frank. THE POLICE FUNCTION. Mineola, N.Y.: Foundation Press, 1971.

1149. Minnick, Wayne C. THE ART OF PERSUASION. Burlington, Mass.: Houghton-Mifflin Co., 1969.

1150. MUNICIPAL POLICE ADMINISTRATION. Santa Cruz, Calif.: Davis Publishing Co., 1972.

1151. National Learning Corporation. POLICEWOMAN: PASSBOOK FOR CIVIL SERVICE EXAMINATIONS. Brooklyn, N.Y.: National Learning Corporation, 1968.

★1152. Niederhoffer, Arthur. BEHIND THE SHIELD: THE POLICE IN URBAN SOCIETY. Garden City, N.Y.: Doubleday and Co., 1967.

1153. Odiorne, George. PERSONNEL ADMINISTRATION BY OBJECTIVES. Homewood, Ill.: Dow Jones-Irwin, 1971.

1154. Otto, Calvin P., and R. O. Glasser. THE MANAGEMENT OF TRAIN-ING: A HANDBOOK FOR TRAINING DIRECTORS. Reading, Mass.: Addison-Wesley Publishing Co., 1970.

1155. Parker, Willard E., and others. FRONT-LINE LEADERSHIP. New York, N.Y.: McGraw-Hill, 1969.

1156. Peel, Roy. THE OMBUDSMAN OR CITIZEN'S DEFENDER: A MODERN INSTITUTION. Philadelphia, Pa.: American Academy of Political and Social Science, 1968.

1157. Pell, Arthur R. POLICE LEADERSHIP. Springfield, Ill.: Charles C. Thomas, 1967.

1158. Pell, Arthur R. RECRUITING AND SELECTING PERSONNEL. New York, N.Y.: Regents Publishing Co., 1969.

1159. Pigors, Paul. PERSONNEL ADMINISTRATION. New York, N.Y.: McGraw-Hill, 1973.

1160. POLICE YEARBOOK. (Annual) Santa Cruz, Calif.: Davis Publishing Co.

1161.   Reeves, Elton. SO YOU WANT TO BE A SUPERVISOR. Riverside, N.J.: American Management Association, 1971.

1162.   Resnicoff, Samuel. THREE HUNDRED FIFTY QUIZZES AND ANSWERS FOR LAW-ENFORCEMENT POSITIONS. New York, N.Y.: Law-Arts Publishing Co., 1969.

1163.   Scheer, Wilbert E. PERSONNEL DIRECTOR'S HANDBOOK. Chicago, Ill.: Dartnell Publishing, 1970.

1164.   Stahl, O. Glenn. PUBLIC PERSONNEL ADMINISTRATION. New York, N.Y.: Harper and Row, 1971.

1165.   Steinmetz, Lawrence. INTERVIEWING SKILLS FOR SUPERVISORY PERSONNEL. Reading, Mass.: Addison-Wesley Publishing Co., 1971.

1166.   Sterling, James. CHANGES IN ROLE CONCEPTS OF POLICE OFFICERS DURING RECRUIT TRAINING. Gaithersburg, Md.: International Association of Chiefs of Police, 1969.

1167.   Stinchcomb, James. OPPORTUNITIES IN A LAW ENFORCEMENT CAREER. New York, N.Y.: Universal Publishing and Distributing, 1971.

1168.   Thompson, Vance. ROOKIE COP'S GUIDEBOOK: HOW TO MAKE A SUCCESS OF YOUR POLICE DEPARTMENT CAREER. Jericho, N.Y.: Exposition Press, 1970.

1169.   U. S. Department of Labor. A HANDBOOK FOR JOB RESTRUCTURING. Washington, D.C.: U. S. Government Printing Office, 1970.

1170.   U. S. Law Enforcement Assistance Administration. PORTABLE POLICE PENSIONS: IMPROVING INTER-AGENCY TRANSFERS. Washington, D.C.: U. S. Government Printing Office, 1972.

1171.   U. S. Law Enforcement Assistance Administration. PSYCHOLOGICAL ASSESSMENT OF PATROLMAN QUALIFICATIONS IN RELATION TO POLICE PERFORMANCE. Washington, D.C.: U. S. Government Printing Office, 1968.

★1172.   Watson, Nelson. POLICE AND THEIR OPINIONS. Gaithersburg, Md.: International Association of Chiefs of Police, 1969.

1173.   THE WAY I SEE IT. (16mm b&w, 23 min.) Beverly Hills, Calif.: Roundtable Films, Inc.

1174.   Weston, Paul. SUPERVISION IN THE ADMINISTRATION OF JUSTICE: POLICE, CORRECTIONS, COURTS. Springfield, Ill.: Charles C. Thomas, 1970.

1175.   Whisenand, Paul M. POLICE SUPERVISION: THEORY AND PRAC-
        TICE. Englewood Cliffs, N.J.: Prentice Hall, 1971.

1176.   Yoder, Dale. PERSONNEL MANAGEMENT AND INDUSTRIAL
        RELATIONS. Englewood Cliffs, N.J.: Prentice Hall, 1970.

PLANNING AND EVALUATION

See also Communications: Data/Visual/   Police Organization
              Voice/Equipment   Police Patrol Function
           Criminal Investigation   Police Traffic Function
           Information: Systems/Software   Public Information and
           Judicial Process   Education
           Personnel Administration   Reference Materials
           Police Equipment   Statistics
           Police Internal Affairs   Support Services
           Police Management   Training

1177.   Adams, Thomas (ed.). CRIMINAL JUSTICE: READINGS. Pacific
        Palisades, Calif.: Goodyear Publishing, 1971.

★1178. Adams, Thomas. LAW ENFORCEMENT: AN INTRODUCTION TO
        THE POLICE ROLE IN THE CRIMINAL JUSTICE SYSTEM.
        Englewood Cliffs, N.J.: Prentice Hall, 1972.

1179.   Ahern, James. POLICE IN TROUBLE: OUR FRIGHTENING
        CRISIS IN LAW ENFORCEMENT. New York, N.Y.: Hawthorn Books,
        1972.

1180.   American Enterprise Institute for Public Policy Research. SPECIAL
        ANALYSIS: COMBATTING CRIME. Washington, D.C.: American
        Enterprise Institute for Public Policy Research, 1967.

1181.   Becker, Harold K. NEW DIMENSIONS IN CRIMINAL JUSTICE.
        Metuchen, N.J.: Scarecrow Press, 1968.

1182.   Biderman, Albert D., and others. REPORT ON A PILOT STUDY IN
        THE DISTRICT OF COLUMBIA ON VICTIMIZATION AND ATTI-
        TUDES TOWARD LAW ENFORCEMENT—FIELD SURVEYS I.
        Washington, D.C.: U. S. Government Printing Office, 1967.

1183.   Blumberg, Abraham S. CRIMINAL JUSTICE. Chicago, Ill.: Quadrangle
        Books, 1967.

1184.   Bouma, D. H., and D. G. Williams. EVALUATION OF A POLICE-
        SCHOOL LIAISON PROGRAM. Springfield, Va.: National Technical
        Information Service, 1970.

1185. Bragdon, Henry, and John C. Pittenger. THE PURSUIT OF JUSTICE: AN INTRODUCTION TO CONSTITUTIONAL RIGHTS. Riverside, N.J.: Macmillan Co., 1970.

★1186. Brandstatter, Arthur, and Allen Hyman. FUNDAMENTALS OF LAW ENFORCEMENT. Riverside, N.J.: Glencoe Press, 1971.

★1187. Casper, J. AMERICAN CRIMINAL JUSTICE: THE DEFENDENT'S PERSPECTIVE. Englewood Cliffs, N.J.: Prentice Hall, 1972.

1188. CED Staff. REDUCING CRIME AND ASSURING JUSTICE. New York, N.Y.: Committee for Economic Development, 1972.

1189. Clift, Raymond E. A GUIDE TO MODERN POLICE THINKING. Buffalo, N.Y.: W. S. Hein and Co., 1970.

1190. Cole, George. CRIMINAL JUSTICE: LAW AND POLITICS. Belmont, Calif.: Duxbury Press, 1972.

1191. Cunningham, W. M. COALESCENCE OF MUNICIPAL POLICE AND FIRE SERVICES: A COMPARISON OF EXPERIENCE. Ann Arbor, Mich.: University Microfilm, 1970.

1192. Dickson, Paul. THINK TANKS. New York, N.Y.: Atheneum Publishers, 1971.

★1193. Eldefonso, Edward. PRINCIPLES OF LAW ENFORCEMENT. New York, N.Y.: John Wiley and Sons, 1968.

1194. Emerson, R. D. AN ECONOMIC ANALYSIS OF THE PROVISION OF POLICE SERVICES. Ann Arbor, Mich.: University Microfilm, 1970.

1195. Foster, Jack Donald. READINGS IN CRIMINAL JUSTICE. Berkeley, Calif.: McCutchan Publishing Corporation, 1969.

★1196. Germann, A. C., and others. INTRODUCTION TO LAW ENFORCE-MENT AND CRIMINAL JUSTICE. Springfield, Ill.: Charles C. Thomas, 1972.

1197. Giertz, J. F. ECONOMIC ANALYSIS OF THE DISTRIBUTION OF POLICE PATROL FORCES. Springfield, Va.: National Technical Information Service, 1970.

1198. Hanna, Donald, and John Kleberg. POLICE RECORDS SYSTEMS FOR THE SMALL DEPARTMENT. Springfield, Ill.: Charles C. Thomas, 1969.

★1199. Hewitt, William. POLICE RECORDS ADMINISTRATION. Rochester, N.Y.: Acqueduct Books, 1968.

1200. International Association of Chiefs of Police. FISCAL MANAGEMENT. Gaithersburg, Md.: International Association of Chiefs of Police, 1968.

1201. International Association of Chiefs of Police. HIGHWAY SAFETY POLICIES FOR POLICE EXECUTIVES. Gaithersburg, Md.: International Association of Chiefs of Police, 1967.

1202. International Association of Chiefs of Police. MODEL RULES AND REGULATIONS: MANUAL OF RULES. Gaithersburg, Md.: International Association of Chiefs of Police, 1967.

1203. International Association of Chiefs of Police. WRITTEN DIRECTIVE SYSTEM. Gaithersburg, Md.: International Association of Chiefs of Police, 1968.

1204. Kakalik, James. AIDS TO DECISION MAKING IN POLICE PATROL: SURVEY RESPONSE. Santa Monica, Calif.: Rand Corporation, 1970.

★1205. Karlen, Delmar. ANGLO-AMERICAN CRIMINAL JUSTICE. New York, N.Y.: Oxford University Press, 1967.

1206. Kimble, Joseph P. AN OUTLINE FOR POLICE ADMINISTRATORS TO ESTABLISH EFFECTIVE TECHNIQUES IN DEALING WITH COMMUNITY TENSIONS AND CIVIL DISTURBANCES. Gaithersburg, Md.: International Association of Chiefs of Police, 1967.

1207. Lenher, John. FLOWCHARTING: AN INTRODUCTORY TEXT AND WORKBOOK. Princeton, N.J.: Auerbach, 1972.

★1208. Leonard, V. A. THE POLICE RECORDS SYSTEM. Springfield, Ill.: Charles C. Thomas, 1970.

★1209. Leonard, V. A., and Harry W. More. THE GENERAL ADMINISTRATION OF CRIMINAL JUSTICE. Mineola, N.Y.: Foundation Press, 1967.

1210. Leonard, V. A. THE POLICE, THE JUDICIARY, AND THE CRIMINAL. Springfield, Ill.: Charles C. Thomas, 1969.

1211. Lyden, Freemont, and Ernest Miller. PLANNING, PROGRAMMING, BUDGETING: A SYSTEMS APPROACH TO MANAGEMENT. Chicago, Ill.: Markham Publishing Co., 1968.

1212. More, Harry. THE NEW ERA OF PUBLIC SAFETY. Springfield, Ill.: Charles C. Thomas, 1970.

1213. Mushkin, Selma J., and John F. Cotton. SHARING FEDERAL FUNDS FOR STATE AND LOCAL NEEDS: GRANTS-IN-AID AND PPB SYSTEMS. New York, N.Y.: Praeger Publishers, 1969.

1214. National Governors' Conference. CORRECTIONS IN THE CRIMINAL JUSTICE SYSTEMS. Chicago, Ill.: National Governors' Conference, 1970.

1215. National Research Council. LONG-RANGE PLANNING FOR URBAN RESEARCH AND DEVELOPMENT: TECHNOLOGICAL CONSIDERATIONS. Washington, D.C.: National Academy of Science, 1969.

1216. Norrgard, David. REGIONAL LAW ENFORCEMENT: A STUDY OF INTERGOVERNMENTAL COOPERATION AND COORDINATION. Chicago, Ill.: Public Administration Service, 1969.

★1217. Oaks, Dallin H. A CRIMINAL JUSTICE SYSTEM AND THE INDIGENT: A STUDY OF CHICAGO AND COOK COUNTY. Chicago, Ill.: University of Chicago Press, 1968.

1218. Pfiffner, John M. THE FUNCTION OF THE POLICE IN A DEMOCRATIC SOCIETY. Berkeley, Calif.: University of California Press, 1967.

1219. Pomrenke, Norman E. LAW ENFORCEMENT MANUAL: RULES AND REGULATIONS. Gaithersburg, Md.: International Association of Chiefs of Police, 1967.

★1220. President's Commission on Law Enforcement and Administration of Justice. THE POLICE: TASK FORCE REPORT. Washington, D.C.: U. S. Government Printing Office, 1967.

1221. Reiss, Albert J., Jr. THE POLICING OF EVERYDAY LIFE, OUR POLICE STANDARDS AND CONDUCT, TOWARD A CIVIL SOCIETY. New Haven, Conn.: Yale University Press, 1969.

★1222. Remington, Frank J. CRIMINAL JUSTICE ADMINISTRATION: MATERIALS AND CASES. Indianapolis, Ind.: Bobbs-Merrill, 1969, (1971 Supplement).

1223. Saphier, Michael. OFFICE PLANNING AND DESIGN. New York, N.Y.: McGraw-Hill, 1968.

★1224. Shoup, Donald C. PROGRAM BUDGETING FOR URBAN POLICE SERVICE. New York, N.Y.: Praeger Publishers, 1971.

1225. Tenzer, A. J., and J. B. Benton. APPLYING THE CONCEPTS OF PROGRAM BUDGETING TO THE NEW YORK CITY POLICE DEPARTMENT. Santa Monica, Calif.: Rand Corporation, 1969.

1226.   Tracey, William R. EVALUATING TRAINING AND DEVELOPMENT
        SYSTEMS. Riverside, N.J.: American Management Association, 1968.

1227.   Turner, William. POLICE ESTABLISHMENT. New York, N.Y.: Tower
        Publications, 1971.

1228.   U. S. Advisory Commission on Intergovernmental Relations. MAKING
        THE SAFE STREETS ACT WORK: AN INTERGOVERNMENTAL
        CHALLENGE. Washington, D.C.: U. S. Government Printing Office,
        1970.

1229.   U. S. Advisory Commission on Intergovernmental Relations. STATE-
        LOCAL RELATIONS IN THE CRIMINAL JUSTICE SYSTEM: A
        COMMISSION REPORT. Washington, D.C.: U. S. Government Print-
        ing Office, 1971.

1230.   U. S. Congress Joint Economic Committee. THE FEDERAL CRIM-
        INAL JUSTICE SYSTEM. Washington, D.C.: U. S. Government Print-
        ing Office, 1970.

1231.   U. S. Law Enforcement Assistance Administration. NATIONAL
        CONFERENCE ON CRIMINAL JUSTICE, JANUARY 23-26, 1973.
        Washington, D.C.: U. S. Department of Justice, 1973.

1232.   U. S. Law Enforcement Assistance Administration. REGIONAL
        CRIMINAL JUSTICE PLANNING. (5 parts.) Washington, D.C.:
        National Association of Counties Research Foundation, 1971.

1233.   U. S. Office of Education. PREPARING EVALUATION REPORTS:
        A GUIDE FOR AUTHORS. Washington, D.C.: U. S. Government
        Printing Office, 1970.

1234.   Vera Institute. THE ADMINISTRATION OF JUSTICE UNDER
        EMERGENCY CONDITIONS. New York, N.Y.: Vera Institute of
        Justice, 1969.

1235.   Weston, Paul. CRIMINAL JUSTICE AND LAW ENFORCEMENT:
        CASES. Englewood Cliffs, N.J.: Prentice Hall, 1972.

★1236. Weston, Paul, and Kenneth Wells. LAW ENFORCEMENT AND
        CRIMINAL JUSTICE: AN INTRODUCTION. Pacific Palisades, Calif.:
        Goodyear Publications, 1972.

1237.   Wholey, Joseph. FEDERAL EVALUATION POLICY: ANALYZING
        THE EFFECTS OF PUBLIC PROGRAMS. Washington, D.C.: Urban
        Institute, 1970.

★1238. Williams, E. W. MODERN LAW ENFORCEMENT AND POLICE
        SCIENCE. Springfield, Ill.: Charles C. Thomas, 1967.

★1239. Wilson, Orlando W. POLICE PLANNING. Springfield, Ill.: Charles C.
        Thomas, 1971.

★1240. Wright, R. Gene, and J. Marco. THE POLICE OFFICER AND CRIM-
        INAL JUSTICE. New York, N.Y.: McGraw-Hill, 1970.

POLICE EQUIPMENT

See also **Communications: Data/Visual/
            Voice/Equipment
        Explosives and Weapons
        Information: Systems/Software
        Planning and Evaluation**

**Police Patrol Functions
Police Traffic Functions
Security Systems
Training**

  1241. American Bar Association. STANDARDS RELATING TO ELEC-
        TRONIC SURVEILLANCE: TENTATIVE DRAFT. Chicago, Ill.:
        American Bar Association, 1968.

  1242. Applegate, Rex. RIOT CONTROL—MATERIAL AND TECHNIQUES.
        Harrisburg, Pa.: Stackpole Co., 1969.

  1243. Barnes, Frank C. CARTRIDGES OF THE WORLD. Chicago, Ill.:
        Follett Publishing Co., 1972.

  1244. Blair, Claude. PISTOLS OF THE WORLD. New York, N.Y.: Viking
        Press, 1969.

★1245. Bristow, Allen. THE SEARCH FOR AN EFFECTIVE POLICE HAND-
        GUN. Springfield, Ill.: Charles C. Thomas, 1972.

  1246. Boothroyd, Geoffrey. THE HANDGUN. New York, N.Y.: Crown Pub-
        lishing Co., 1970.

  1247. Carroll, John M. THE THIRD LISTENER: PERSONAL ELECTRONIC
        ESPIONAGE. New York, N.Y.: E. P. Dutton and Co., 1969.

  1248. Chilton's AUTOMOBILE REPAIR MANUAL. Philadelphia, Pa.: Chilton
        Book Co., 1972.

★1249. Coates, J. F. NONLETHAL WEAPONS FOR USE BY U.S. LAW
        ENFORCEMENT OFFICERS. Springfield, Va.: National Technical
        Information Service, 1967.

  1250. Cramer, James. UNIFORMS OF THE WORLD'S POLICE WITH BRIEF
        DATA ON ORGANIZATION, SYSTEMS, AND WEAPONS. Spring-
        field, Ill.: Charles C. Thomas, 1968.

1251. Crockett, Thompson S. POLICE CHEMICAL AGENTS MANUAL. Gaithersburg, Md.: International Association of Chiefs of Police, 1970.

1252. EAVESDROPPING. (Cassette tape, 26 min.) North Hollywood, Calif.: Center for Cassette Studies.

1253. Grennell, D., and M. Williams. LAW ENFORCEMENT HANDGUN DIGEST. Santa Cruz, Calif.: Davis Publishing Co., 1972.

1254. Hogg, I. V. MILITARY PISTOLS AND REVOLVERS: THE HAND-GUNS OF THE TWO WORLD WARS. New York, N.Y.: Arco Publishing Co., 1970.

1255. Josserand, Michel, and Jan Stevenson. PISTOLS, REVOLVERS AND AMMUNITION. New York, N.Y.: Crown Publishing Co., 1972.

1256. Keith, Elmer. SHOTGUNS. Harrisburg, Pa.: Stackpole Co., 1967.

1257. Larson, E. Dixon. COLT TIPS. Union City, Tenn.: Pioneer Press, 1972.

1258. Lowry, E. D. INTERIOR BALLISTICS: HOW A GUN CONVERTS CHEMICAL ENERGY INTO PROJECTILE MOTION. Garden City, N.Y.: Doubleday and Co., 1968.

★1259. National Fire Protection Association. MANUAL OF HAZARDOUS CHEMICAL REACTIONS. Boston, Mass.: National Fire Protection Association, 1968.

1260. National Rifle Association. NRA POLICE FIREARMS INSTRUCTOR MANUAL. Washington, D.C.: National Rifle Association of America, 1968.

1261. NEW WEAPONS AGAINST CRIME. (16mm color, 26 min.) New York, N.Y.: Columbia Broadcasting System.

1262. Pierce, E. T., and M. A. McPherson. EMERGENCY VEHICLE WARN-ING DEVICES—INTERIM REVIEW OF STATE-OF-THE-ART RELA-TIVE TO PERFORMANCE STANDARDS. Washington, D.C.: National Bureau of Standards, 1971.

★1263. President's Commission on Law Enforcement and Administration of Justice. SCIENCE AND TECHNOLOGY: TASK FORCE REPORT. Washington, D.C.: U. S. Government Printing Office, 1967.

1264. RECORDS. (Sound filmstrip, color.) Gaithersburg, Md.: International Association of Chiefs of Police.

★1265. Roberts, Willis, and Allen Bristow. INTRODUCTION TO MODERN POLICE FIREARMS. Riverside, N.J.: Glencoe Press, 1969.

1266. Smith, Joseph. SMALL ARMS OF THE WORLD: A BASIC MANUAL OF SMALL ARMS. Harrisburg, Pa.: Stackpole Co., 1969.

1267. Smith, W. H. B. BOOK OF PISTOLS AND REVOLVERS. Harrisburg, Pa.: Stackpole Co., 1968.

1268. U. S. Federal Communications Commission. RADIO EQUIPMENT LIST: EQUIPMENT ACCEPTABLE FOR LICENSING. Washington, D.C.: U. S. Federal Communications Commission, 1972.

1269. U. S. Law Enforcement Assistance Administration. BATTERIES USED WITH LAW ENFORCEMENT COMMUNICATIONS EQUIPMENT: COMPARISON AND PERFORMANCE CHARACTERISTICS. Washington, D.C.: U. S. Government Printing Office, 1972.

1270. U. S. Law Enforcement Assistance Administration. EMERGENCY WARNING DEVICES: INTERIM REVIEW OF THE STATE-OF-THE-ART RELATIVE TO PERFORMANCE STANDARDS. Washington, D.C.: U. S. Department of Justice, 1972.

1271. U. S. Law Enforcement Assistance Administration. STANDARDS ON THE BALLISTIC RESISTANCE OF POLICE BODY ARMOR. Washington, D.C.: U. S. Government Printing Office, 1972.

POLICE—INTERNAL AFFAIRS

See also **Personnel Administration**   **Police Organization**
Planning and Evaluation   **Police Patrol Function**
Police Equipment   **Police Traffic Function**
Police Management

1272. Bordua, David J. (ed.). THE POLICE: SIX SOCIOLOGICAL ESSAYS. New York, N.Y.: John Wiley and Sons, 1967.

1273. Gray, Ed. THE ENEMY IN THE STREETS: POLICE MALPRACTICE IN AMERICA. Garden City, N.Y.: Doubleday and Co., 1972.

1274. Klein, Herbert T. THE POLICE—DAMNED IF THEY DO—DAMNED IF THEY DON'T. New York, N.Y.: Crown Publishers, 1968.

1275. Littman, Sol. THE POLICEMAN LOOKS AT HIMSELF. Philadelphia, Pa.: Anti-Defamation League, 1967.

1276. POLICING THE POLICE. (Cassette tape, 54 min.) North Hollywood, Calif.: Center for Cassette Studies.

1277. PROFESSIONAL POLICE ETHICS. (Sound filmstrip, color.) Gaithersburg, Md.: International Association of Chiefs of Police.

1278. THE SERVE AND PROTECT FALLACY. (Cassette tape, 27 min.) North Hollywood, Calif.: Center for Cassette Studies.

1279. Sokol, Ronald P. THE LAW-ABIDING POLICEMAN. Charlottsville, Va.: Michie Co., 1969.

POLICE MANAGEMENT

See also Communications: Data/Visual/ Voice/Equipment
Information: Systems/Software
Personnel Administration
Planning and Evaluation
Police Equipment
Police Internal Affairs
Police Organization

Police Patrol Function
Police Traffic Function
Public Information and Education
Research and Development
Statistics
Support Services
Training

1280. Barnard, Chester. THE FUNCTIONS OF THE EXECUTIVE. Cambridge, Mass.: Harvard University Press, 1968.

1281. Becker, Harold K. ISSUES IN POLICE ADMINISTRATION. Metuchen, N.J.: Scarecrow Press, 1970.

1282. Blake, Robert Rogers, and Jane S. Mouton. CORPORATE EXCEL-LENCE THROUGH GRID ORGANIZATION DEVELOPMENT. Houston, Tex.: Gulf Publishing Co., 1968.

★1283. Bristow, Allen. EFFECTIVE POLICE MANPOWER UTILIZATION. Springfield, Ill.: Charles C. Thomas, 1969.

1284. Cornell University Medical College. THE TREATMENT OF MASS CIVILIAN CASUALTIES IN A NATIONAL EMERGENCY. Ithaca, N.Y.: Cornell University Press, 1968.

1285. Eastman, George D. MUNICIPAL POLICE ADMINISTRATION. Washington, D.C.: International City Management Association, 1970.

1286. Elliott, J. F., and Thomas Sardino. CRIME CONTROL TEAM: AN EXPERIMENT IN MUNICIPAL POLICE DEPARTMENT MANAGE-MENT AND OPERATIONS. Springfield, Ill.: Charles C. Thomas, 1971.

1287. Etzioni, Amitai. READINGS ON MODERN ORGANIZATIONS. Englewood Cliffs, N.J.: Prentice Hall, 1969.

1288. Garb, Solomon, and Evelyn Eng. DISASTER HANDBOOK. New York, N.Y.: Springer Publishing Co., 1969.

★1289. Gourley, Gerald. EFFECTIVE MUNICIPAL POLICE ORGANIZA-
TION. Riverside, N.J.: Glencoe Press, 1970.

★1290. Hanna, Donald G., and William D. Gentel. A GUIDE TO PRIMARY
POLICE MANAGEMENT CONCEPTS. Springfield, Ill.: Charles C.
Thomas, 1971.

1291. Healy, Richard J. EMERGENCY AND DISASTER PLANNING. New
York, N.Y.: John Wiley and Sons, 1969.

1292. Heyel, Carl. HANDBOOK OF MODERN MANAGEMENT AND
ADMINISTRATIVE SERVICES. New York, N.Y.: McGraw-Hill, 1972.

1293. International City Managers' Association. MUNICIPAL POLICE
ADMINISTRATION. Washington, D.C.: International City Managers'
Association, 1969.

1294. Irwin, Bud. A POLICEMAN'S LOT. Cranbury, N.Y.: A. S. Barnes and
Co., 1968.

1295. Jenkins, Herbert. KEEPING THE PEACE: A POLICE CHIEF LOOKS
AT HIS JOB. New York, N.Y.: Harper and Row, 1970.

1296. Kassoff, Norman C. THE POLICE MANAGEMENT SYSTEM.
Gaithersburg, Md.: International Association of Chiefs of Police, 1967.

1297. Kazmier, Leonard J. PRINCIPLES OF MANAGEMENT: A PROGRAM
FOR SELF-INSTRUCTION. New York, N.Y.: McGraw-Hill, 1969.

1298. Kennedy, W. C. POLICE DEPARTMENT IN NATURAL DISASTER
OPERATIONS: DISASTER RESEARCH CENTER REPORT SERIES
NO. 6. Springfield, Va.: National Technical Information Service, 1969.

★1299. Kenney, John P. POLICE OPERATIONS: POLICIES AND PRO-
CEDURES: 400 FIELD SITUATIONS WITH SOLUTIONS. Springfield, Ill.: Charles C. Thomas, 1968.

★1300. Koontz, Harold. PRINCIPLES OF MANAGEMENT. New York, N.Y.:
McGraw-Hill, 1972.

1301. Lane, Roger. POLICING THE CITY. Cambridge, Mass.: Harvard University Press, 1967.

1302. Lazzaro, Victor (ed.). SYSTEMS AND PROCEDURES: A HANDBOOK FOR
BUSINESS AND INDUSTRY. Englewood Cliffs, N.J.: Prentice Hall, 1968.

★1303. Leonard, V. A. THE POLICE ENTERPRISE: ITS ORGANIZATION
AND MANAGEMENT. Springfield, Ill.: Charles C. Thomas, 1969.

1304. Levinson, Harry. THE EXCEPTIONAL EXECUTIVES: A PSYCHO-
LOGICAL CONCEPTION. Cambridge, Mass.: Harvard University
Press, 1968.

1305. McGregor, Douglas. THE PROFESSIONAL MANAGER. New York,
N.Y.: McGraw-Hill, 1967.

1306. Murray, Joseph A. POLICE ADMINISTRATION AND CRIMINAL
INVESTIGATION. New York, N.Y.: Arco Publishing Co., 1968.

1307. Newman, William H., and others. THE PROCESS OF MANAGEMENT:
CONCEPTS, BEHAVIOR AND PRACTICE. Englewood Cliffs, N.J.:
Prentice Hall, 1971.

1308. Nielsen, Swen. GENERAL ORGANIZATIONAL AND ADMINISTRA-
TIVE CONCEPTS FOR UNIVERSITY POLICE. Springfield, Ill.:
Charles C. Thomas, 1971.

★1309. President's Commission on Law Enforcement and Administration of
Justice. EFFECTIVE POLICE ORGANIZATION AND MANAGE-
MENT CONSULTANT PAPER. Washington, D.C.: U. S. Government
Printing Office, 1967.

1310. Reynolds, Russel B. THE OFFICER'S GUIDE. Harrisburg, Pa.:
Stackpole Co., 1967.

1311. RULES, REGULATIONS, PROCEDURES. (Sound filmstrip, color.)
Gaithersburg, Md.: International Association of Chiefs of Police.

1312. Sayles, Leonard, and Margaret Chandler. MANAGING LARGE
SYSTEMS: ORGANIZATIONS FOR THE FUTURE. New York, N.Y.:
Harper and Row, 1971.

1313. Schoderbek, Peter. MANAGEMENT SYSTEMS. New York, N.Y.: John
Wiley and Sons, 1971.

★1314. Schwartz, Louis B., and Stephen R. Goldstein. LAW ENFORCEMENT
HANDBOOK FOR POLICE. St. Paul, Minn.: West Publishing Co.,
1970.

1315. Smith, Bruce. THE STATE POLICE: ORGANIZATION AND ADMIN-
ISTRATION. Montclair, N.J.: Patterson Smith Publishing Corporation, 1969.

1316. Warner, Kenneth O., and Mary L. Hennessy. PUBLIC MANAGEMENT
AT THE BARGAINING TABLE. Chicago, Ill.: Public Personnel
Association, 1967.

★1317.   Wilson, James. VARIETIES OF POLICE BEHAVIOR: THE MANAGE-
        MENT OF LAW AND ORDER IN EIGHT COMMUNITIES. Cambridge,
        Mass.: Harvard University Press, 1968.

 1318.   Wilson, Orlando, and Roy McLaren. POLICE ADMINISTRATION.
        New York, N.Y.: McGraw-Hill, 1972.

POLICE ORGANIZATION

See also **Communications: Data/Visual/**   **Police Patrol Function**
      Voice/Equipment   **Police Traffic Function**
Education   **Public Information and**
Information: Systems/Software   **Education**
Personnel Administration   **Research and Development**
Planning and Evaluation   **Statistics**
Police Equipment   **Support Services**
Police Internal Affairs   **Training**
Police Management

 1319.   International Association of Chiefs of Police. STANDARDS FOR THE
        STAFFING AND ORGANIZATION OF MUNICIPAL NARCOTICS
        AND DANGEROUS DRUG ENFORCEMENT UNITS. Gaithersburg,
        Md.: International Association of Chiefs of Police, 1970.

 1320.   J. EDGAR HOOVER'S FBI. (Cassette tape, 44 min.) North Hollywood,
        Calif.: Center for Cassette Studies.

 1321.   Kassoff, Norman C. ORGANIZATION CONCEPTS. Gaithersburg, Md.:
        International Association of Chiefs of Police, 1967.

 1322.   ORGANIZATIONAL CONCEPTS. (Sound filmstrip, color.) Gaithers-
        burg, Md.: International Association of Chiefs of Police.

★1323.   Schultz, Donald O., and L. A. Norton. POLICE OPERATIONAL
        INTELLIGENCE. Springfield, Ill.: Charles C. Thomas, 1971.

 1324.   Sullivan, Francis C., and others. THE ADMINISTRATION OF CRIM-
        INAL JUSTICE. Mineola, N.Y.: Foundation Press, 1969.

 1325.   U. S. Law Enforcement Assistance Administration. PRIVATE POLICE
        IN THE UNITED STATES: FINDINGS AND RECOMMENDA-
        TIONS. (5 vols.) Washington, D.C.: U. S. Government Printing Office,
        1972.

See also Communications: Data/Visual/
  Voice/Equipment
Crime Deterrence and Prevention
Criminal Investigation
Criminalistics
Criminology
Explosives and Weapons
Information: Systems/Software
Organized Crime
Personnel Administration

Planning and Evaluation
Police Equipment
Police Management
Police Organization
Police Traffic Function
Riot Control and Urban
  Disorders
Student Disorders
Training

*1326. Adams, Thomas E. POLICE PATROL: TACTICS AND TECH-NIQUES. Englewood Cliffs, N.J.: Prentice Hall, 1971.

1327. AGGRESSIVE PATROL. (Sound filmstrip, color.) Gaithersburg, Md.: International Association of Chiefs of Police.

1328. ARREST AND SEARCH. (Cassette tape, 27 min.) North Hollywood, Calif.: Center for Cassette Studies.

1329. BEAT PATROL AND OBSERVATION. (16mm color, 22 min.) Sacramento, Calif.: California Peace Officers Association.

1330. Bristow, Allen P. FIELD INTERROGATION. Springfield, Ill.: Charles C. Thomas, 1970.

1331. Campbell, Judith. POLICE HORSES. Cranbury, N.J.: A. S. Barnes Co., 1968.

1332. Casey, Patrick. DETERMINING POLICE PATROL CAR REQUIRE-MENTS BY COMPUTER SIMULATION. Tempe, Ariz.: Arizona State University Press, 1968.

1333. Chapman, Samuel G. DOGS IN POLICE WORK: A SUMMARY OF EXPERIENCE IN GREAT BRITAIN AND THE UNITED STATES. Chicago, Ill.: Public Administration Service, 1969.

1334. Chapman, Samuel. POLICE PATROL READINGS. Springfield, Ill.: Charles C. Thomas, 1970.

1335. CRIME SCENE PROCEDURES. (Sound filmstrip, color.) Gaithersburg, Md.: International Association of Chiefs of Police.

1336. Cunningham, Donald, and others. A READING APPROACH TO PROFESSIONAL POLICE WRITING. Springfield, Ill.: Charles C. Thomas, 1972.

*1337. Dienstein, William. HOW TO WRITE A NARRATIVE INVESTIGA-TION REPORT. Springfield, Ill.: Charles C. Thomas, 1969.

1338. DISTURBANCE CALLS: GENERAL #1. (16mm or videotape, color, 20 min. each.) Chicago, Ill.: Motorola Systems, Inc.

1339. Elliott, James, and Thomas Sardino. CRIME CONTROL TEAM: AN EXPERIMENT IN MUNICIPAL POLICE DEPARTMENT MANAGE-MENT AND OPERATIONS. Springfield, Ill.: Charles C. Thomas, 1971.

1340. EVERY HOUR—EVERY DAY. (16mm color, 28 min.) Gaithersburg, Md.: International Association of Chiefs of Police.

1341. FELONY ARRESTS. (Sound filmstrip, color.) Gaithersburg, Md.: International Association of Chiefs of Police.

1342. FELONY-IN-PROGRESS CALLS. (Sound filmstrip, color.) Gaithers-burg, Md.: International Association of Chiefs of Police.

★1343. Fennessy, E. F., and T. Hamilton. STUDY OF THE PROBLEM OF HOT PURSUIT BY THE POLICE. Springfield, Va.: National Technical Information Service, 1970.

1344. FIELD INQUIRY. (Sound filmstrip, color.) Gaithersburg, Md.: International Association of Chiefs of Police.

1345. FORESTS OF THE NIGHT. (16mm color, 15 min.) Gaithersburg, Md.: International Association of Chiefs of Police.

★1346. Gammage, Allen Z. BASIC POLICE REPORT WRITING. Springfield, Ill.: Charles C. Thomas, 1970.

1347. GATHERING INFORMATION FROM PEOPLE. (Sound filmstrip, color.) Gaithersburg, Md.: International Association of Chiefs of Police.

★1348. Gourley, G. Douglas, and Allen P. Bristow. PATROL ADMINISTRA-TION. Springfield, Ill.: Charles C. Thomas, 1971.

1349. HANDLING DISTURBANCE CALLS. (Sound filmstrip, color.) Gaithersburg, Md.: International Association of Chiefs of Police.

★1350. Holcomb, Richard L. POLICE PATROL. Springfield, Ill.: Charles C. Thomas, 1971.

1351. International Association of Chiefs of Police. THE PATROL OPER-ATION. Gaithersburg, Md.: International Association of Chiefs of Police, 1970.

1352. Larson, Richard. URBAN POLICE PATROL ANALYSIS. Cambridge, Mass.: Massachusetts Institute of Technology Press, 1972.

★1353. McArthur, Jack. POLICE PATROL POINTERS. Riverside, N.J.:
        Glencoe Press, 1969.

★1354. Nelson, John G. PRELIMINARY INVESTIGATION AND POLICE
        REPORTING: A COMPLETE GUIDE TO POLICE WRITTEN
        COMMUNICATION. Riverside, N.J.: Glencoe Press, 1970.

 1355. O'Connor, George W., and Charles G. Vanderbosch. THE PATROL
        OPERATION. Gaithersburg, Md.: International Association of Chiefs
        of Police, 1970.

 1356. ONE-MAN PATROL. (Sound filmstrip, color.) Gaithersburg, Md.:
        International Association of Chiefs of Police.

 1357. PATROL PROCEDURES I-VIOLENT CRIMES. (16mm or videotape,
        color, 20 min. each.) Chicago, Ill.: Motorola Systems, Inc.

 1358. Patterson, Frank M., and Patrick D. Smith. A MANUAL OF POLICE
        REPORT WRITING. Springfield, Ill.: Charles C. Thomas, 1968.

 1359. Payton, George T. PATROL PROCEDURE. Los Angeles, Calif.: Legal
        Book Store, 1971.

 1360. PLAY IT COOL—A QUESTION OF ATTITUDES. (16mm color,
        15 min.) New York, N.Y.: Association Instructional Materials.

 1361. THE PRELIMINARY INVESTIGATION. (Sound filmstrip, color.)
        Gaithersburg, Md.: International Association of Chiefs of Police.

 1362. Radano, Gene. WALKING THE BEAT: A NEW YORK POLICEMAN
        TELLS WHAT IT'S LIKE ON HIS SIDE OF THE LAW. Lakewood,
        Ohio: World Publishing Co., 1968.

 1363. RECOGNIZING AND PROTECTING THE CRIME SCENE. (16mm
        color, 14 min.) Sacramento, Calif.: California Peace Officers
        Association.

 1364. REPORT WRITING. (Sound filmstrip, color.) Gaithersburg, Md.:
        International Association of Chiefs of Police.

 1365. Robinson, Barry, and Martin J. Dain. ON THE BEAT: POLICEMEN
        AT WORK. New York, N.Y.: Harcourt, Brace and World, 1968.

 1366. SEARCHING ARRESTED PERSONS. (Sound filmstrip, color.)
        Gaithersburg, Md.: International Association of Chiefs of Police.

 1367. STAY ALERT—STAY ALIVE. (16mm color, 20 min.) Washington,
        D.C.: Federal Bureau of Investigation.

1368. STOPPING THE FELONY SUSPECT. (Sound filmstrip, color.) Gaithersburg, Md.: International Association of Chiefs of Police.

1369. Tiffany, Lawrence P., and others. DETECTION OF CRIME: STOPPING AND QUESTIONING, SEARCH AND SEIZURE, ENCOURAGEMENT AND ENTRAPMENT. Waltham, Mass.: Little, Brown and Co., 1967.

1370. TRANSPORTING PRISONERS. (Sound filmstrip, color.) Gaithersburg, Md.: International Association of Chiefs of Police.

1371. U. S. Law Enforcement Assistance Administration. PROJECT SKY KNIGHT: A DEMONSTRATION IN AERIAL SURVEILLANCE AND CRIME CONTROL. Washington, D.C.: U. S. Department of Justice, 1968.

1372. U. S. Law Enforcement Assistance Administration. THE USE OF PROBABILITY THEORY IN THE ASSIGNMENT OF POLICE PATROL AREAS. Washington, D.C.: U. S. Law Enforcement Assistance Administration, 1970.

1373. U. S. Law Enforcement Assistance Administration. THE UTILIZATION OF HELICOPTERS FOR POLICE AIR MOBILITY. Washington, D.C.: U. S. Government Printing Office, 1971.

1374. USE OF HANDCUFFS. (Sound filmstrip, color.) Gaithersburg, Md.: International Association of Chiefs of Police.

1375. USE OF THE POLICE BATON. (Sound filmstrip, color.) Gaithersburg, Md.: International Association of Chiefs of Police.

★1376. Whisenand, Paul M. PATROL OPERATIONS. Englewood Cliffs, N.J.: Prentice Hall, 1971.

POLICE TRAFFIC FUNCTION

See also Communications: Data/Visual/   Personnel Administration
            Voice/Equipment   Planning and Evaluation
         Crime Deterrence and Prevention   Police Equipment
         Criminal Investigation   Police Management
         Criminalistics   Police Organization
         Information: Systems/Software   Training

1377. THE ACCIDENT SCENE. (Sound filmstrip, color.) Gaithersburg, Md.: International Association of Chiefs of Police.

1378. Allen, Merrill J. VISION AND HIGHWAY SAFETY. Philadelphia, Pa.: Chilton Book Co., 1970.

1379. Arthur D. Little, Inc. COST-EFFECTIVENESS IN TRAFFIC
       SAFETY. New York, N.Y.: Praeger Publishers, 1968.

1380. AUTO THEFT. (Sound filmstrip, color.) Gaithersburg, Md.: Interna-
       tional Association of Chiefs of Police.

1381. Collins, James C., and Joe L. Morris. HIGHWAY COLLISION ANAL-
       YSIS. Springfield, Ill.: Charles C. Thomas, 1967.

1382. DIRECTING TRAFFIC. (Sound filmstrip, color.) Gaithersburg, Md.:
       International Association of Chiefs of Police.

1383. Drew, Donald. TRAFFIC FLOW THEORY AND CONTROL. New
       York, N.Y.: McGraw-Hill, 1968.

1384. DRIVING UNDER THE INFLUENCE. (Sound filmstrip, color.)
       Gaithersburg, Md.: International Association of Chiefs of Police.

1385. EMERGENCY TRAFFIC CONTROL. (Sound filmstrip, color.)
       Gaithersburg, Md.: International Association of Chiefs of Police.

★1386. Filkins, L. D. ALCOHOL ABUSE AND TRAFFIC SAFETY—A STUDY
       OF FATALITIES, DW1 OFFENDERS, ALCOHOLICS, AND COURT
       RELATED TREATMENT APPROACHES. Springfield, Va.: National
       Technical Information Service, 1970.

★1387. Gardiner, John A. TRAFFIC AND THE POLICE: VARIATIONS IN
       LAW ENFORCEMENT POLICY. Cambridge, Mass.: Harvard University
       Press, 1969.

1388. Gurdjian, Elisha S., and others. IMPACT INJURY AND CRASH PRO-
       TECTION. Springfield, Ill.: Charles C. Thomas, 1970.

1389. HIT AND RUN INVESTIGATION. (Sound filmstrip, color.) Gaithers-
       burg, Md.: International Association of Chiefs of Police.

1390. National Highway Safety Bureau. HIGHWAY SAFETY PROGRAM
       STANDARDS. Washington, D.C.: U. S. Government Printing Office,
       1969.

1391. National Safety Council. MANUAL ON CLASSIFICATION OF
       MOTOR VEHICLE TRAFFIC ACCIDENTS. Chicago, Ill.: National
       Safety Council, 1970.

1392. Parry, Meyer H. AGGRESSION ON THE ROAD. New York, N.Y.:
       Barnes and Noble, 1968.

1393. Roberts, H. J. THE CAUSES, ECOLOGY AND PREVENTION OF
       TRAFFIC ACCIDENTS: WITH EMPHASIS UPON TRAFFIC

MEDICINE, EPIDEMIOLOGY, SOCIOLOGY AND LOGISTICS. Springfield, Ill.: Charles C. Thomas, 1971.

1394. Rodgers, Lionel M., and L. J. Sands. AUTOMOBILE TRAFFIC SIGNAL CONTROL SYSTEMS. Philadelphia, Pa.: Chilton Book Co., 1969.

1395. ROUTINE STOPS. (16mm color, 15 min.) Los Angeles, Calif.: Charles Cahill and Associates.

1396. SKID MARK EVIDENCE. (Sound filmstrip, color.) Gaithersburg, Md.: International Association of Chiefs of Police.

1397. Smith, R. Dean, and David Espic. GUIDELINES FOR POLICE SERVICES ON CONTROLLED ACCESS ROADWAYS. Gaithersburg, Md.: International Association of Chiefs of Police, 1968.

1398. THE TRAFFIC VIOLATOR. (Sound filmstrip, color.) Gaithersburg, Md.: International Association of Chiefs of Police.

1399. U. S. Congress (House). AUTOMOBILE INSURANCE STUDY. Washington, D.C.: U. S. Government Printing Office, 1967.

1400. U. S. Federal Highway Administration. MANUAL OF UNIFORM TRAFFIC CONTROL DEVICES. Washington, D.C.: U. S. Governm Printing Office, 1971.

1401. U. S. National Highway Traffic Safety Administration. PERFORM- ANCE DATA: NEW 1972 PASSENGER CARS AND MOTORCYCLES. Washington, D.C.: U. S. Government Printing Office, 1972.

1402. U. S. President's Task Force on Highway Safety. MOBILITY WITH- OUT MAYHEM: THE REPORT. Washington, D.C.: U. S. Government Printing Office, 1970.

1403. U. S. Transportation Department. SAFETY FOR MOTOR VEHICLES IN USE: REPORT. Washington, D.C.: U. S. Government Printing Office, 1968.

1404. Vanderbosch, Charles G. TRAFFIC SUPERVISION. Gaithersburg, Md.: International Association of Chiefs of Police, 1969.

1405. Weiers, Ronald M. LICENSED TO KILL—THE INCOMPETENT AMERICAN MOTORIST AND HOW HE GOT THAT WAY. Philadelphia, Pa.: Chilton Book Co., 1968.

★1406. Weston, Paul B. POLICE TRAFFIC CONTROL FUNCTION. Spring- field, Ill.: Charles C. Thomas, 1972.

See also Behavioral and Social Science   Jails
Community Based Corrections: Judicial Process
   Adult/Juvenile   Laws and Statutes
Correctional Institutions:
   Adult/Juvenile

1407. American Bar Association. STANDARDS RELATING TO PROBA-
TION: TENTATIVE DRAFT. Chicago, Ill.: American Bar Association, 1970.

★1408. Arnold, William R. JUVENILES ON PAROLE: A SOCIOLOGICAL
PERSPECTIVE. Westminster, Md.: Random House, 1970.

1409. AUTOMATIC PROBATION. (Cassette tape, 51 min.) North Hollywood, Calif.: Center for Cassette Studies.

★1410. Carter, Robert, and Leslie Wilkins. PROBATION AND PAROLE:
SELECTED READINGS. New York, N.Y.: John Wiley and Sons, 1970.

★1411. Dressler, David. PRACTICE AND THEORY OF PROBATION AND
PAROLE. Irvington, N.Y.: Columbia University Press, 1969.

1412. Evrard, Franklin. SUCCESSFUL PAROLE. Springfield, Ill.: Charles
C. Thomas, 1971.

1413. Glaser, Daniel. THE EFFECTIVENESS OF A PRISON AND PAROLE
SYSTEM. Indianapolis, Ind.: Bobbs-Merrill, 1969.

★1414. Keve, Paul W. IMAGINATIVE PROGRAMMING IN PROBATION
AND PAROLE. Minneapolis, Minn.: University of Minnesota Press,
1967.

1415. Manella, R. L. POST-INSTITUTIONAL SERVICES FOR DELIN-
QUENT YOUTH. Washington, D.C.: U. S. Government Printing Office,
1968.

1416. Newman, Charles. PERSONNEL PRACTICES IN ADULT PAROLE
SYSTEMS. Springfield, Ill.: Charles C. Thomas, 1971.

1417. Newman, Charles. SOURCEBOOK ON PROBATION, PAROLE AND
PARDONS. Springfield, Ill.: Charles C. Thomas, 1968.

1418. U. S. Administrative Office of the Courts, Probation Division.
PERSONS UNDER THE SUPERVISION OF THE FEDERAL PROBA-
TION SYSTEM. Washington, D.C.: U. S. Government Printing Office,
1968.

1419. U. S. Office of Juvenile Delinquency and Youth Development. THE CRISIS OF QUALIFIED MANPOWER FOR CRIMINAL JUSTICE: AN ANALYTIC ASSESSMENT WITH GUIDELINES FOR NEW POLICY—PROBATION AND PAROLE. Washington, D.C.: U. S. Government Printing Office, 1969.

1420. Young, Pauline V. SOCIAL TREATMENT IN PROBATION AND DELINQUENCY. Montclair, N.J.: Patterson-Smith, 1969.

PROSECUTION

See also **Civil Rights**   **Judicial Process**
            Classification of: Crime/Offenders   **Laws and Statutes**

1421. American Bar Association. STANDARDS RELATIVE TO THE PROSECUTION FUNCTION AND THE DEFENSE FUNCTION: TENTATIVE DRAFT. Chicago, Ill.: American Bar Association, 1970.

1422. George, James. THE PROSECUTOR'S SOURCEBOOK. New York, N.Y.: Practicing Law Institute, 1969.

1423. Healy, Patrick. THE PROSECUTOR'S DESKBOOK. Chicago, Ill.: National District Attorneys Association, 1971.

★1424. Miller, Frank W. PROSECUTION: THE DECISION TO CHARGE A SUSPECT WITH A CRIME. Boston, Mass.: Little, Brown and Co., 1969.

1425. Mills, James. THE PROSECUTOR. New York, N.Y.: Farrar, Straus, Giroux, 1969.

1426. Spellman, Howard Hilton. DIRECT EXAMINATION OF WITNESSES. Englewood Cliffs, N.J.: Prentice Hall, 1968.

PUBLIC INFORMATION AND EDUCATION

See also **Community Relations**   **Research and Development**
            Drug: Information/Treatment   **Training**
            Education

1427. Marx, Jerry. OFFICER TELL YOUR STORY: A GUIDE TO POLICE PUBLIC RELATIONS. Springfield, Ill.: Charles C. Thomas, 1967.

1428. THE POLICE IMAGE. (Sound filmstrip, color.) Gaithersburg, Md.: International Association of Chiefs of Police.

1429. Schreiber, Flora Rheta. A JOB WITH A FUTURE IN LAW ENFORCE-
MENT AND RELATED FIELDS. New York, N.Y.: Grosset and
Dunlap, 1970.

1430. Whittemore, L. H. COP: A CLOSEUP OF VIOLENCE AND TRAGEDY.
New York, N.Y.: Fawcett World Library, 1970.

REFERENCE MATERIAL

See also **Communications: Data/Visual/**   **Personnel Administration**
       Voice/Equipment   **Planning and Evaluation**
     Information: Systems/Software   **Research and Development**

1431. Abrams, Charles, and R. Kolodny. THE LANGUAGE OF CITIES:
A GLOSSARY OF TERMS. New York, N.Y.: Viking Press, 1971.

1432. Advena, Jean. DRUG ABUSE BIBLIOGRAPHY FOR 1971. Troy,
N.Y.: Whitston Publishing Co., 1972.

1433. American Correctional Association. CORRECTIONS: A BIBLIOG-
RAPHY. Washington, D.C.: American Correctional Association, 1971.

1434. Banki, I. S. DICTIONARY OF ADMINISTRATION AND SUPER-
VISION. Santa Cruz, Calif.: Davis Publishing Co., 1971.

1435. Becker, Harold. LAW ENFORCEMENT: A SELECTED BIBLIOG-
RAPHY. Metuchen, N.J.: Scarecrow Press, 1968.

1436. Bristow, Allen. POLICE FILM GUIDE. Walteria, Calif.: Police
Research Associates, 1968.

1437. Carpenter, Glenn. LAW ENFORCEMENT TRAINING MATERIALS
DIRECTORY. Washington, D.C.: Capitol Publishers, 1969.

1438. Fricke, Charles. 5000 CRIMINAL DEFINITIONS: TERMS AND
PHRASES. Los Angeles, Calif.: Legal Book Corporation, 1968.

1439. Gale Research Company. ENCYCLOPEDIA OF ASSOCIATIONS.
(3 vols.) Detroit, Mich.: Gale Research, 1972.

1440. Hewitt, William H. BIBLIOGRAPHY OF POLICE ADMINISTRA-
TION: PUBLIC SAFETY AND CRIMINOLOGY TO JULY 1, 1965.
Springfield, Ill.: Charles C. Thomas, 1967.

1441. International Association of Chiefs of Police. INTERNATIONAL
BIBLIOGRAPHY OF SELECTED POLICE LITERATURE. Gaithersburg, Md.: International Association of Chiefs of Police, 1968.

1442. International Association of Chiefs of Police. LAW ENFORCEMENT EDUCATION DIRECTORY. Gaithersburg, Md.: International Association of Chiefs of Police, 1970.

1443. International Association of Chiefs of Police. THE POLICE WEAPONS CENTER DATA SERVICE. Gaithersburg, Md.: International Association of Chiefs of Police, 1972.

1444. Landy, Eugene. UNDERGROUND DICTIONARY. New York, N.Y.: Simon and Schuster, 1971.

1445. Limbacher, James. A REFERENCE GUIDE TO AUDIOVISUAL INFORMATION. New York, N.Y.: Bowker, 1972.

1446. Lingeman, Richard. DRUGS FROM A TO Z: A DICTIONARY. New York, N.Y.: McGraw-Hill, 1969.

1447. Menditto, Joseph. DRUGS OF ADDICTION AND NON-ADDICTION, THEIR USE AND ABUSE: A COMPREHENSIVE BIBLIOGRAPHY. Troy, N.Y.: Whitston Publishers, 1970.

1448. Milton, C. H., and B. Battista. POLICE FILM CATALOG. Gaithersburg, Md.: International Association of Chiefs of Police, 1970.

1449. National Audio-Visual Association, Inc. AUDIO-VISUAL EQUIPMENT DIRECTORY. (Annual.) Fairfax, Va.: National Audio-Visual Association, Inc.

1450. National Council on Crime and Delinquency. CRIMINOLOGICAL RESEARCH INSTITUTES IN THE UNITED STATES AND CANADA. New York, N.Y.: National Council on Crime and Delinquency, 1969.

1451. Paradis, Adrian. THE LABOR REFERENCE BOOK. Philadelphia, Pa.: Chilton Book Co., 1972.

1452. Porter, Dorothy. THE NEGRO IN THE UNITED STATES: A SELECTED BIBLIOGRAPHY. Washington, D.C.: U. S. Government Printing Office, 1970.

1453. Renetcky, Alvin, and Jean Aroeste. ANNUAL REGISTER OF GRANT SUPPORT. Los Angeles, Calif.: Academic Media, 1972.

1454. Roberts, Henry. ROBERT'S RULES OF ORDER. West Caldwell, N.J.: William Morrow, 1971.

1455. Salottolo, A. Lawrence. MODERN POLICE SERVICE ENCYCLO-PEDIA. New York, N.Y.: Arco Publishing Co., 1970.

1456. Schmeckebier, Laurence, and Roy Fastin. GOVERNMENT PUBLICA-
TIONS AND THEIR USE. Washington, D.C.: Brookings Institution,
1969.

1457. Schmidt, Jacob Edward. POLICE MEDICAL DICTIONARY. Springfield, Ill.: Charles C. Thomas, 1968.

1458. Shapiro, Irving. DICTIONARY OF LEGAL TERMS. Jamaica, N.Y.:
Gould Publications, 1969.

1459. Smith, Emerson. GLOSSARY OF COMMUNICATIONS. Chicago, Ill.:
Telephony Publication Corporation, 1971.

1460. Stecher, Paul. THE MERCK INDEX: AN ENCYCLOPEDIA OF
CHEMICALS AND DRUGS. Rahway, N.J.: Merck and Co., 1968.

1461. Steindler, R. A. FIREARMS DICTIONARY. Harrisburg, Pa.: Stackpole
Co., 1970.

1462. Taintor, Sarah Augusta. THE SECRETARY'S HANDBOOK: A MAN-
UAL OF CORRECT USAGE. Riverside, N.J.: Macmillan Co., 1969.

1463. U. S. Bureau of Prisons. CORRECTIONAL EDUCATION: A BIBLIOG-
RAPHY. Washington, D.C.: U. S. Bureau of Prisons, 1972.

1464. U. S. Law Enforcement Assistance Administration. DOCUMENT
RETRIEVAL INDEX. Washington, D.C.: National Criminal Justice
Reference Service, U. S. Department of Justice. (Quarterly).

1465. U. S. Law Enforcement Assistance Administration. LIBRARY BOOK
CATALOG. (Author, title, subject in 3 vols.) Washington, D.C.: U. S.
Government Printing Office, 1972.

1466. U. S. National Clearinghouse for Drug Abuse Information. DRUG
DEPENDENCE AND ABUSE: A SELECTED BIBLIOGRAPHY.
Washington, D.C.: U. S. Government Printing Office, 1971.

1467. U. S. National Institute of Mental Health. BIBLIOGRAPHY ON
DRUG DEPENDENCE AND ABUSE 1928-1966. Washington, D.C.:
U. S. Government Printing Office, 1969.

1468. U. S. National Institute of Mental Health. DIRECTORY OF NAR-
COTIC ADDICTION TREATMENT AGENCIES IN THE UNITED
STATES. Washington, D.C.: U. S. Government Printing Office, 1970.

1469. U. S. National Institute of Mental Health. SELECTED SOURCES OF
INEXPENSIVE MENTAL HEALTH MATERIALS. Washington, D.C.:
U. S. Government Printing Office, 1972.

1470.   U. S. Office of Economic Opportunity. CATALOG OF FEDERAL DOMESTIC ASSISTANCE. Washington, D.C. U. S. Government Printing Office, 1970.

1471.   U. S. Public Health Service. NATIONAL DRUG CODE DIRECTORY. Washington, D.C.: U. S. Government Printing Office, 1971.

1472.   Urban Institute. DIRECTORY OF UNIVERSITY URBAN RESEARCH CENTERS. New York, N.Y.: Urban Institute, 1971.

1473.   Watanabe, Tomio. ATLAS OF LEGAL MEDICINE. Philadelphia, Pa.: J. B. Lippincott Co., 1968.

1474.   Wells, Dorothy. DRUG EDUCATION: A BIBLIOGRAPHY OF AVAILABLE INEXPENSIVE MATERIALS. Metuchen, N.J.: Scarecrow Press, 1972.

1475.   Wynkoop, Sally. SUBJECT GUIDE TO GOVERNMENT REFERENCE BOOKS. Littleton, Colo.: Libraries Unlimited, 1972.

RESEARCH AND DEVELOPMENT

See also Communications: Data/Visual/   Reference Material
                 Voice/Equipment   Statistics
           Information: Systems/Software   Support Services
           Planning and Evaluation   Training
           Police Equipment

1476.   Blalock, Hubert. AN INTRODUCTION TO SOCIAL RESEARCH. Englewood Cliffs, N.J.: Prentice Hall, 1970.

1477.   Blalock, Hubert, and Ann Blalock. METHODOLOGY IN SOCIAL RESEARCH. New York, N.Y.: McGraw-Hill, 1968.

1478.   Buckley, Walter. MODERN SYSTEMS RESEARCH FOR THE BEHAVIORAL SCIENTIST: A SOURCEBOOK. Chicago, III.: Aldine/Atherton, 1968.

1479.   Denzin, Norman. THE RESEARCH ACT: A THEORETICAL INTRODUCTION TO SOCIOLOGICAL METHODS. Chicago, III.: Aldine/Atherton, 1970.

1480.   Dubois, Philip. RESEARCH STRATEGIES FOR EVALUATING TRAINING. Chicago, III.: Rand McNally, 1970.

1481.   Isaac, Stephen. HANDBOOK IN RESEARCH AND EVALUATION. San Diego, Calif.: Robert R. Knapp, 1971.

1482. Shaw, Lynette, and H. S. Sichel. ACCIDENT PRONENESS. Elmsford, N.Y.: Pergamon Press, 1971.

★1483. U. S. Law Enforcement Assistance Administration. A LOOK AT CRIMINAL JUSTICE RESEARCH. Washington, D.C.: U. S. Government Printing Office, 1971.

1484. Wilsnack, R. W. COMPREHENSIVE LAW AND ORDER ASSISTANCE RESEARCH AND DEVELOPMENT (CLOARAD) PROGRAM: FINAL REPORT—REVISED. Springfield, Va.: National Technical Information Service, 1971.

RIOT CONTROL AND URBAN DISORDERS

See also **Behavioral and Social Science**   **Police Equipment**
Crime Deterrence and Prevention   **Police Management**
Criminology   **Police Organization**
Explosives and Weapons   **Police Patrol Function**
Juvenile Delinquency   **Student Disorders**
Planning and Evaluation   **Training**

1485. Applegate, Rex. RIOT CONTROL: MATERIAL AND TECHNIQUES. Santa Cruz, Calif.: Davis Publishing Co., 1969.

★1486. Bassiouni, M. Cherif. THE LAW OF DISSENT AND RIOTS. Springfield, Ill.: Charles C. Thomas, 1971.

1487. BATTLE OF EAST ST. LOUIS. (16mm b&w, 40 min.) New York, N.Y.: Anti-Defamation League of B'nai B'rith.

★1488. Bedau, Hugo Adam. CIVIL DISOBEDIENCE: THEORY AND PRACTICE. Indianapolis, Ind.: Bobbs-Merrill Co., 1969.

1489. Bottoms, A. M. POLICE AND CIVIL DISORDER. Evanston, Ill.: Northwestern University Press, 1969.

1490. Caffi, Andrea. A CRITIQUE OF VIOLENCE. Indianapolis, Ind.: Bobbs-Merrill Co., 1970.

1491. Chevigny, Paul. COPS AND REBELS: A STUDY OF PROVOCATION. New York, N.Y.: Pantheon, 1972.

1492. Cohen, Nathan Ed. THE LOS ANGELES RIOTS: A SOCIO-PSYCHOLOGICAL STUDY. New York, N.Y.: Praeger Publishers, 1970.

1493. Connery, Robert. URBAN RIOTS: VIOLENCE AND SOCIAL CHANGE. Westminster, Md.: Random House, 1969.

1494. CROWD CONTROL. (Sound filmstrip, color.) Gaithersburg, Md.:
       International Association of Chiefs of Police.

1495. Endleman, Shalom. VIOLENCE IN THE STREETS. Chicago, Ill.:
       Quadrangle Books, 1968.

1496. Farmer, David J. CIVIL DISORDER CONTROL: A PLANNING
       PROGRAM OF MUNICIPAL COORDINATION AND COOPERA-
       TION. Chicago, Ill.: Public Administration Service, 1968.

1497. Fogelson, Robert M., and Richard Rubinstein (eds.). MASS VIO-
       LENCE IN AMERICA: THE LOS ANGELES RIOTS. New York,
       N.Y.: Arno Press, 1969.

★1498. Fogelson, Robert M. VIOLENCE AS PROTEST: A STUDY OF
       RIOTS AND GHETTOS. Garden City, N.J.: Doubleday and Co.,
       1971.

1499. Gilbert, Ben W. TEN BLOCKS FROM THE WHITE HOUSE:
       ANATOMY OF THE WASHINGTON RIOTS OF 1968. New York,
       N.Y.: Praeger Publishers, 1968.

1500. Glick, Edward Bernard. PEACEFUL CONFLICT: THE NON-
       MILITARY USE OF THE MILITARY. Harrisburg, Pa.: Stackpole
       Co., 1967.

1501. Harris, Dale. VIOLENCE IN CONTEMPORARY AMERICAN
       SOCIETY. University Park, Pa.: Pennsylvania State University Press,
       1969.

1502. Hendel, Samuel. THE POLITICS OF CONFRONTATION. New York,
       N.Y.: Appleton-Century-Crofts, 1971.

1503. Hersey, John. THE ALGIERS MOTEL INCIDENT. New York, N.Y.:
       Alfred A. Knopf, 1968.

1504. Higham, Robin. BAYONETS IN THE STREETS: THE USE OF
       TROOPS IN CIVIL DISTURBANCES. Lawrence, Kan.: University
       Press of Kansas, 1969.

1505. Hormachea, C. R. CONFRONTATION, VIOLENCE AND THE
       POLICE. Rockleigh, N.Y.: Holbrook Press, 1971.

1506. Janowitz, Morris. SOCIAL CONTROL OF ESCALATED RIOTS.
       Chicago, Ill.: University of Chicago Press, 1968.

1507. Lincoln, James H. THE ANATOMY OF A RIOT: A DETROIT
       JUDGE'S REPORT. New York, N.Y.: McGraw-Hill, 1968.

★1508. Lipsky, M. LAW AND ORDER: POLICE ENCOUNTERS. Chicago, Ill.: Aldine/Atherton, 1970.

★1509. Locke, Hubert G. THE DETROIT RIOT OF 1967. Detroit, Mich.: Wayne State University Press, 1969.

1510. Lowi, Theodore. THE POLITICS OF DISORDER. Scranton, Pa.: Basic Books, 1971.

1511. Masotti, Louis H., and Don R. Bowen. RIOTS AND REBELLIONS— CIVIL VIOLENCE IN THE URBAN COMMUNITY. Beverly Hills, Calif.: Sage Publications, 1968.

1512. Masotti, Louis H. SHOOT-OUT IN CLEVELAND—BLACK MILI- TANTS AND THE POLICE, JULY 23, 1968. New York, N.Y.: Praeger Publishers, 1969.

1513. Methvin, Eugene H. THE RIOT MAKERS: THE TECHNOLOGY OF SOCIAL DEMOLITION. New Rochelle, N.Y.: Arlington House, 1970.

★1514. Mitchell, J. Paul. RACE RIOTS IN BLACK AND WHITE. Englewood Cliffs, N.J.: Prentice Hall, 1970.

★1515. Momboisse, Raymond M. BLUEPRINT OF REVOLUTION: THE REBEL, THE PARTY, THE TECHNIQUES OF REVOLT. Springfield, Ill.: Charles C. Thomas, 1970.

★1516. Momboisse, Raymond M. RIOTS, REVOLTS AND INSURREC- TIONS. Springfield, Ill.: Charles C. Thomas, 1970.

1517. Neuberg, A. ARMED INSURRECTION. Dunmore, Pa.: St. Martin's Press, 1971.

1518. Oppenheimer, Martin. THE URBAN GUERRILLA. Chicago, Ill.: Quadrangle Books, 1969.

1519. Pinkney, Alphonso. THE AMERICAN WAY OF VIOLENCE. West- minster, Md.: Random House, 1972.

1520. Platt, Anthony. THE POLITICS OF RIOT COMMISSIONS, 1917- 1970: A COLLECTION OF OFFICIAL REPORTS AND CRITICAL ESSAYS. Riverside, N.J.: Macmillan Co., 1971.

1521. THE POLICE FILM. (16mm color, 51 min.) Mt. Vernon, N.Y.: CCM Films, Inc.

1522. REMEDY FOR RIOT. (16mm b&w, 37 min.) New York, N.Y.: Anti-Defamation League of B'nai B'rith.

1523. THE RIOT COMMISSION REPORT. (Cassette tape, 47 min.) North Hollywood, Calif.: Center for Cassette Studies.

1524. RIOT-CONTROL WEAPONS. (16mm b&w, 6 min.) San Francisco, Calif.: San Francisco Newsreel.

1525. Rosenthal, C. R. PHASES OF CIVIL DISTURBANCES—CHARACTER-ISTICS AND PROBLEMS. Springfield, Va.: National Technical Information Service, 1969.

1526. Rossi, Peter H. GHETTO REVOLTS. Chicago, Ill.: Aldine/Atherton, 1970.

1527. Samuels, D. W., and D. O. Egner. RIOT CONTROL—ANALYSIS AND CATALOG: FINAL REPORT. Springfield, Va.: National Technical Information Service, 1969.

1528. Sasso, Carmen D. COPING WITH PUBLIC EMPLOYEE STRIKES. Chicago, Ill.: Public Personnel Association, 1970.

1529. Schultz, John. NO ONE WAS KILLED: CONVENTION WEEK, CHICAGO—AUGUST 1968. Chicago, Ill.: Follett Publishing Co., 1969.

1530. Shuman, Samuel I. LAW AND DISORDER: THE LEGITIMATION OF DIRECT ACTION AS AN INSTRUMENT OF SOCIAL POLICY. Detroit, Mich.: Wayne State University Press, 1971.

1531. Singer, Benjamin D., and others. BLACK RIOTERS: SOCIOLOGICAL AND COMMUNICATIONS FACTORS IN THE DETROIT RIOT OF 1967. Lexington, Mass.: Lexington Books, 1970.

1532. SOME TO DEMONSTRATE—SOME TO DESTROY. (16mm color, 23 min.) Gaithersburg, Md.: International Association of Chiefs of Police.

1533. Stein, David Lewis. LIVING THE REVOLUTION: THE YIPPIES IN CHICAGO. Indianapolis, Ind.: Bobbs-Merrill, 1969.

★1534. Towler, Juby E. POLICE ROLE IN RACIAL CONFLICTS. Springfield, Ill.: Charles C. Thomas, 1969.

1535. U. S. Bureau of Prisons. EMERGENCY DETENTION MANUAL: TEMPORARY DETENTION OF CIVIL DISTURBANCE VIOLATORS PRIOR TO COURT ACTION. Washington, D.C.: U. S. Bureau of Prisons, 1969.

1536. U. S. Committee on the Judiciary. ASSAULTS ON LAW ENFORCE-MENT OFFICERS. Washington, D.C.: U.S. Government Printing Office, 1971.

1537.   U.S. Committee on Un-American Activities. GUERRILLA WARFARE ADVOCATES IN THE UNITED STATES. Washington, D.C.: U. S. Government Printing Office, 1968.

1538.   U. S. Committee on Un-American Activities. SUBVERSIVE INFLU-ENCES IN RIOTS, LOOTING, AND BURNING: HEARINGS BEFORE...90th CONGRESS, 1st SESSION...1968. Washington, D.C.: U. S. Government Printing Office, 1968.

★1539.   U. S. National Advisory Commission on Civil Disorder. REPORT OF THE NATIONAL ADVISORY COMMISSION ON CIVIL DISORDERS. Washington, D.C.: U. S. Government Printing Office, 1968.

1540.   U. S. National Commission on Prevention of Violence. MIAMI REPORT: THE REPORT OF THE MIAMI STUDY TEAM ON CIVIL DISTURBANCES IN MIAMI, FLORIDA DURING THE WEEK OF AUGUST 5, 1968. Washington, D.C.: U. S. Government Printing Office, 1969.

1541.   U. S. National Commission on Prevention of Violence. THE POLITICS OF PROTEST, VIOLENT ASPECTS OF PROTEST, AND CONFRON-TATION. Washington, D.C.: U. S. Government Printing Office, 1969.

★1542.   U. S. National Commission on Prevention of Violence. TO ESTAB-LISH JUSTICE, TO INSURE DOMESTIC TRANQUILITY—FINAL REPORT. Washington, D.C.: U. S. Government Printing Office, 1969.

1543.   U. S. National Commission on Prevention of Violence. VIOLENCE IN AMERICA: HISTORICAL AND COMPARATIVE PERSPEC-TIVES. Washington, D.C.: U. S. Government Printing Office, 1969.

1544.   U. S. Youth Development and Delinquency Prevention Administration. YOUTH AND VIOLENCE. Washington, D.C.: U. S. Government Print-ing Office, 1970.

1545.   Urban American, Inc. ONE YEAR LATER: AN ASSESSMENT OF THE NATION'S RESPONSE TO THE CRISIS DESCRIBED BY THE NATIONAL ADVISORY COMMISSION ON CIVIL DISORDERS. New York, N.Y.: Praeger Publishers, 1969.

1546.   VIOLENT AMERICA. (Cassette tape, 45 min.) North Hollywood, Calif.: Center for Cassette Studies.

1547.   Walker, Daniel. RIGHTS IN CONFLICT: CHICAGO DURING THE WEEK OF THE DEMOCRATIC NATIONAL CONVENTION OF 1968. Washington, D.C.: U. S. Government Printing Office, 1969.

1548.   WATTS: RIOT OR REVOLT? (16mm b&w, 45 min.) New York, N.Y.: Anti-Defamation League of B'nai B'rith.

*1549. Westley, William A. VIOLENCE AND THE POLICE: A SOCIOLOGI-
        CAL STUDY OF LAW, CUSTOM, AND MORALITY. Cambridge,
        Mass.: Massachusetts Institute of Technology Press, 1970.

1550.   Whittaker, Charles E., and S. Coffin. LAW, ORDER AND CIVIL
        DISOBEDIENCE. Washington, D.C.: American Enterprise Institute
        for Public Policy, 1967.

1551.   THE WHOLE WORLD IS WATCHING. (16mm color, 30 min.)
        Gaithersburg, Md.: International Association of Chiefs of Police.

1552.   Wright, Nathan, Jr. READY TO RIOT. New York, N.Y.: Holt,
        Rinehart and Winston, 1970.

1553.   Zinn, Howard. DISOBEDIENCE AND DEMOCRACY: NINE FALLA-
        CIES OF LAW AND ORDER. Westminster, Md.: Random House, 1968.

SECURITY SYSTEMS

See also Behavioral and Social Science Information: Systems/
          Communications: Data/Visual/   Software
             Voice/Equipment   Planning and Evaluation
          Crime Deterrence and   Police Equipment
             Prevention   Training

1554.   Brann. Donald. HOW TO INSTALL PROTECTIVE ALARM DEVICES.
        Briarcliff Manor, N.Y.: Directions Simplified, 1972.

1555.   Cole, Richard B. THE APPLICATION OF SECURITY SYSTEMS
        AND HARDWARE. Springfield, Ill.: Charles C. Thomas, 1970.

1556.   Cunningham, John E. SECURITY ELECTRONICS. Indianapolis, Ind.:
        H. W. Sams, 1970.

1557.   Curtis, S. J. SECURITY CONTROL: INTERNAL THEFT. New York,
        N.Y.: Chain Store Publishers, 1972.

1558.   Healy, Richard. DESIGN FOR SECURITY. New York, N.Y.: John
        Wiley and Sons, 1968.

1559.   Healy, Richard, and Timothy Walsh. INDUSTRIAL SECURITY
        MANAGEMENT: A COST EFFECTIVE APPROACH. Riverside, N.J.:
        American Management Association, 1971.

1560.   Hemphill, Charles. SECURITY FOR BUSINESS AND INDUSTRY.
        Homewood, Ill.: Dow Jones-Irwin, 1971.

*1561. Momboisse, Raymond M. INDUSTRIAL SECURITY FOR STRIKES, RIOTS, AND DISASTERS. Springfield, Ill.: Charles C. Thomas, 1968.

1562. Peel, John Donald. THE STORY OF PRIVATE SECURITY. Springfield, Ill.: Charles C. Thomas, 1971.

1563. Post, Richard S. SECURITY ADMINISTRATION: AN INTRODUCTION. Springfield, Ill.: Charles C. Thomas, 1970.

*1564. Tobias, Marc Weber. LOCKS, SAFES, AND SECURITY: A HANDBOOK FOR LAW ENFORCEMENT PERSONNEL. Springfield, Ill.: Charles C. Thomas, 1971.

1565. Wels, Byron. FIRE AND THEFT SECURITY SYSTEM. Blue Ridge Summit, Pa.: Tab Books, 1971.

STATISTICS

See also **Classification of: Crime/Offenders   Planning and Evaluation
Communications: Data/Visual/   Reference
Voice/Equipment   Research and Development
Information: Systems/Software   Training**

1566. Smith, G. W. STATISTICAL ANALYSIS OF PUBLIC DEFENDER ACTIVITIES. Springfield, Va.: National Technical Information Service, 1970.

1567. U. S. Federal Bureau of Investigation. UNIFORM CRIME REPORTS FOR THE UNITED STATES. (Annual) Washington, D.C.: U. S. Government Printing Office.

1568. U. S. Law Enforcement Assistance Administration. EXPENDITURE AND EMPLOYMENT DATA FOR THE CRIMINAL JUSTICE SYSTEM 1969-70. Washington, D.C.: U. S. Government Printing Office, 1972.

1569. Walker, Nigel. CRIMES, COURTS AND FIGURES. Baltimore, Md.: Penguin Books, 1971.

1570. American Bar Association. REPORT OF THE COMMISSION ON CAMPUS GOVERNMENT AND STUDENT DISSENT. Chicago, Ill.: American Bar Association, 1970.

1571. Bardis, Panos. ENCYCLOPEDIA OF CAMPUS UNREST. Jericho, N.Y.: Exposition Press, 1971.

1572. Becker, Howard. CAMPUS POWER STRUGGLE. Chicago, Ill.: Aldine/ Atherton, 1970.

1573. Bell, Daniel, and Irving Kristol. CONFRONTATION: THE STUDENT REBELLION AND THE UNIVERSITIES. New York, N.Y.: Basic Books, 1969.

1574. Bloomberg, Edward. STUDENT VIOLENCE. Washington, D.C.: Public Affairs Press, 1970.

★1575. Califano, Joseph A., Jr. THE STUDENT REVOLUTION: A GLOBAL CONFRONTATION. New York, N.Y.: W. W. Norton and Co., 1970.

1576. THE DISSENSION OF YOUTH. (Cassette tape, 28 min.) North Hollywood, Calif.: Center for Cassette Studies.

1577. Eszterhas, Joe. THIRTEEN SECONDS: CONFRONTATION AT KENT STATE. New York, N.Y.: Dodd, Mead, 1970.

1578. Foley, James A., and Robert K. Foley. THE COLLEGE SCENE: STUDENTS TELL IT LIKE IT IS. New York, N.Y.: Cowles Book Co., 1970.

1579. Foster, Julian, and Durward Long. PROTEST: STUDENT ACTIVISM IN AMERICA. West Caldwell, N.J.: William Morrow and Co., 1970.

★1580. Gardner, E. S. COPS ON CAMPUS AND CRIME IN THE STREET. New York, N.Y.: Pocket Books, 1970.

1581. Glazer, Nathan. REMEMBERING THE ANSWERS: ESSAYS ON THE AMERICAN STUDENT REVOLT. New York, N.Y.: Basic Books, 1970.

1582. Goldman, Ronald. ANGRY ADOLESCENTS. Beverly Hills, Calif.: Sage Publications, 1969.

1583. Harris, Janet. STUDENTS IN REVOLT. New York, N.Y.: McGraw-Hill, 1970.

1584. Holmes, Grace W. (ed.). STUDENT PROTEST AND THE LAW. Ann Arbor, Mich.: Institute of Continuing Legal Education, 1969.

★1585. Kelman, Steven. PUSH COMES TO SHOVE: THE ESCALATION OF STUDENT PROTEST. Boston, Mass.: Houghton-Mifflin, 1970.

1586. Kennan, George F. DEMOCRACY AND THE STUDENT LEFT. Waltham, Mass.: Little, Brown and Co., 1968.

1587. Kobetz, R. W. CAMPUS UNREST—DIALOGUE OR DESTRUCTION? Gaithersburg, Md.: International Association of Chiefs of Police, 1970.

1588. Libarle, Marc, and Tom Seligson. THE HIGH SCHOOL REVOLU-TIONARIES. Westminster, Md.: Random House, 1970.

★1589. Lipset, Seymour Martin, and P. G. Altback (eds.). STUDENTS IN REVOLT. Boston, Mass.: Beacon Press, 1970.

1590. McEvoy, James, and Abraham Miller. BLACK POWER AND STUDENT REBELLION: CONFLICT ON THE AMERICAN CAMPUS. Belmont, Calif.: Wadsworth Publishing, 1969.

1591. Michener, James. KENT STATE—WHAT HAPPENED AND WHY. Westminster, Md.: Random House, 1971.

1592. Nichols, David C., and Olive Mills. THE CAMPUS AND THE RACIAL CRISIS. Washington, D.C.: American Council on Education, 1970.

1593. Nichols, David C. (ed.). PERSPECTIVES ON CAMPUS TENSIONS: PAPERS PREPARED FOR THE SPECIAL COMMITTEE ON CAMPUS TENSIONS. Washington, D.C.: American Council on Education, 1970.

1594. Orrick, William. SHUT IT DOWN: A COLLEGE IN CRISIS—SAN FRANCISCO STATE COLLEGE, OCTOBER, 1968. Washington, D.C.: U. S. Government Printing Office, 1969.

1595. Schaap, Dick. TURNED ON. New York, N.Y.: Norton and Co., 1967.

1596. Toole, K. Ross. THE TIME HAS COME. West Caldwell, N.J.: William Morrow, 1971.

★1597. U. S. Center for Studies in Crime and Delinquency. National Institute of Mental Health. YOUTH IN TURMOIL: AMERICA'S CHANGING

YOUTH CULTURES AND STUDENT PROTEST MOVEMENTS. Washington, D.C.: U. S. Government Printing Office, 1970.

1598. U. S. Committee on the Judiciary. EXTENT OF SUBVERSION IN CAMPUS DISORDERS. Washington, D.C.: U. S. Government Printing Office, 1969.

1599. U. S. Congress (House). ANATOMY OF A REVOLUTIONARY MOVE-MENT: STUDENTS FOR A DEMOCRATIC SOCIETY. Washington, D.C.: U. S. Government Printing Office, 1971.

SUPPORT SERVICES

See also Alcoholism
Behavioral and Social Science
Criminology
Drug: Information/Treatment
Judicial Process

Juvenile Delinquency
Laws and Statutes
Personnel Administration
Planning and Evaluation
Training

1600. Adams, Brian C. MEDICAL IMPLICATIONS OF KARATE BLOWS. Cranbury, N.J.: A. S. Barnes and Co., 1969.

1601. Allen, Richard C., and others. READINGS IN LAW AND PSY-CHIATRY. Baltimore, Md.: Johns Hopkins Press, 1968.

1602. Batchelder, Richard L., and James H. Hardy. USING SENSITIVITY TRAINING AND THE LABORATORY METHOD: AN ORGANIZA-TIONAL CASE STUDY IN THE DEVELOPMENT OF HUMAN RESOURCES. New York, N.Y.: Associated Press, 1968.

1603. Bergin, Allen, and Sol Garfield. HANDBOOK OF PSYCHOTHERAPY AND BEHAVIOR CHANGE—AN EMPIRICAL ANALYSIS. New York, N.Y.: John Wiley and Sons, 1970.

1604. Biggs, John. THE GUILTY MIND: PSYCHIATRY AND THE LAW OF HOMICIDE. Baltimore, Md.: Johns Hopkins Press, 1967.

1605. Bour, H., and I. M. Ledingham. CARBON MONOXIDE POISONING. New York, N.Y.: American Elsevier Publishers, 1967.

*1606. Cronbach, Lee J. ESSENTIALS OF PSYCHOLOGICAL TESTING. New York, N.Y.: Harper and Row, 1970.

1607. Gradwohl, Rutherford B. LEGAL MEDICINE. Baltimore, Md.: Williams and Wilkins Co., 1968.

1608. Guttmacher, Manfred S. THE ROLE OF PSYCHIATRY IN LAW. Springfield, Ill.: Charles C. Thomas, 1968.

★1609. Halleck, Seymour L., and Walter Bromberg. PSYCHIATRIC ASPECTS OF CRIMINOLOGY. Springfield, Ill.: Charles C. Thomas, 1968.

★1610. Halleck, Seymour L. PSYCHIATRY AND THE DILEMMAS OF CRIME: A STUDY OF CAUSES, PUNISHMENT AND TREATMENT. New York, N.Y.: Harper and Row, 1967.

★1611. Katz, Jay. PSYCHOANALYSIS, PSYCHIATRY AND LAW. Riverside, N.J.: Macmillan Co., 1967.

1612. MacDonald, John M. PSYCHIATRY AND THE CRIMINAL: A GUIDE TO PSYCHIATRIC EXAMINATIONS FOR THE CRIMINAL COURTS. Springfield, Ill.: Charles C. Thomas, 1969.

1613. Miller, Frank. THE MENTAL HEALTH PROCESS. Mineola, N.Y.: Foundation Press, 1971.

1614. National Fire Protection Association. FIRE PROTECTION HANDBOOK. Boston, Mass.: National Fire Protection Association, 1969.

1615. Polier, Justine Wise. THE RULE OF LAW AND THE ROLE OF PSYCHIATRY. Baltimore, Md.: Johns Hopkins Press, 1968.

★1616. Reiser, Martin. THE POLICE DEPARTMENT PSYCHOLOGIST. Springfield, Ill.: Charles C. Thomas, 1972.

1617. Singer, Jerome. THE CONTROL OF AGGRESSION AND VIOLENCE: COGNITIVE AND PHYSIOLOGICAL FACTORS. New York, N.Y.: Academic Press, 1971.

1618. Ziskin, Jay. COPING WITH PSYCHIATRIC AND PSYCHOLOGICAL TESTIMONY. Beverly Hills, Calif.: Law and Psychology Press, 1970.

TRAINING

★1619. American National Red Cross. BASIC FIRST AID. Garden City, N.Y.: Doubleday and Co., 1971.

1620. American Society for Training and Development. TRAINING AND DEVELOPMENT HANDBOOK. New York, N.Y.: McGraw-Hill, 1967.

1621. Bartlett, Eric. JUDO AND SELF-DEFENSE. New York, N.Y.: Arco Books, 1971.

1622. Benjamin, Bry, and Annette F. Benjamin. IN CASE OF EMERGENCY: WHAT TO DO UNTIL THE DOCTOR ARRIVES. Garden City, N.Y.: Doubleday and Co., 1970.

1623. Chayet, Neil L. LEGAL IMPLICATIONS OF EMERGENCY CARE. New York, N.Y.: Appleton-Century-Croft, 1968.

1624. Clark, D. Cecil. USING INSTRUCTIONAL OBJECTIVES IN TEACHING. Glenview, Ill.: Scott Foresman and Co., 1972.

1625. CONTROLLING SERIOUS BLEEDING. (Sound filmstrip, color.) Gaithersburg, Md.: International Association of Chiefs of Police.

1626. DEFENSIVE DRIVING I, II, III. (16mm or videotape, color, 20 min. each.) Chicago, Ill.: Motorola Systems, Inc.

1627. DEFENSIVE TACTICS. (16mm color, 17 min.) Washington, D.C.: Federal Bureau of Investigation.

1628. DEFENSIVE TACTICS I, II, III. (16mm or videotape, color, 20 min. each.) Chicago, Ill.: Motorola Systems, Inc.

1629. Dudycha, George. PSYCHOLOGY FOR LAW ENFORCEMENT OFFICERS. Springfield, Ill.: Charles C. Thomas, 1971.

1630. Ellison, Bob. THIS BOOK CAN SAVE YOUR LIFE. Bergenfield, N.J.: New American Library, 1968.

1631. EMERGENCY CARE OF FRACTURES. (Sound filmstrip, color.) Gaithersburg, Md.: International Association of Chiefs of Police.

1632. Epstein, Charlotte. INTERGROUP RELATIONS FOR POLICE OFFICERS. New York, N.Y.: Hafner, 1970.

1633. Feldman, Stanley, and Harry Ellis. PRINCIPLES OF RESUSCITATION. Philadelphia, Pa.: F. A. Davis Co., 1967.

1634. Florio, A. E., and George T. Stafford. SAFETY EDUCATION. New York, N.Y.: McGraw-Hill, 1969.

1635. Galvin, J. J., and L. Karacki. MANPOWER AND TRAINING IN CORRECTIONAL INSTITUTIONS. Washington, D.C.: American Correctional Association, 1969.

1636.   Gardner, Alvin. PARAMEDICAL PATHOLOGY: FUNDAMENTALS OF PATHOLOGY FOR THE ALLIED MEDICAL OCCUPATIONS. Springfield, Ill.: Charles C. Thomas, 1972.

1637.   Geesink, Anton. GO-KYO PRINCIPLES OF JUDO. New York, N.Y.: Arco Publishing Co., 1968.

1638.   Goodbody, John. THE JAPANESE FIGHTING ARTS. Cranbury, N.J.: A. S. Barnes and Co., 1969.

1639.   Goodwin, Larry G., and Thomas Koehring. CLOSED-CIRCUIT TELEVISION PRODUCTION TECHNIQUES. Indianapolis, Ind.: Howard W. Sams Co., 1970.

1640.   Greenbank, Anthony. THE BOOK OF SURVIVAL. New York, N.Y.: Harper and Row, 1968.

1641.   Hafen, Brent, and others. FIRST AID: CONTEMPORARY PRACTICES AND PRINCIPLES. Minneapolis, Minn.: Burgess, 1972.

1642.   Hair, Robert, and Sam Sinclair. HOW TO PROTECT YOURSELF TODAY. New York, N.Y.: Stein and Day, 1970.

★1643.   Hansen, David, and Thomas Culley. THE POLICE TRAINING OFFICER. Springfield, Ill.: Charles C. Thomas, 1972.

1644.   Harris, R. N. POLICE ACADEMY—A PSYCHO-STRUCTURAL ANALYSIS. Springfield, Va.: National Technical Information Service, 1970.

1645.   Hatsumi, Masaaki, and Quinton Chambers. STICK FIGHTING: TECHNIQUES OF SELF-DEFENSE. Palo Alto, Calif.: Kodansha International, U.S.A., 1971.

1646.   Heimstra, Norman W. INJURY CONTROL IN TRAFFIC SAFETY. Springfield, Ill.: Charles C. Thomas, 1970.

1647.   Hoffman, Robert N. DRIVER EVALUATION. Cranbury, N.J.: A. S. Barnes, 1968.

1648.   IDENTIFICATION AND CARE OF THE DIABETIC. (Sound filmstrip, color.) Gaithersburg, Md.: International Association of Chiefs of Police.

1649.   International Association of Chiefs of Police. POLICE REFERENCE NOTEBOOK. Gaithersburg, Md.: International Association of Chiefs of Police, 1970.

1650. International Association of Chiefs of Police. POLICE REFERENCE NOTEBOOK: INSTRUCTOR'S GUIDE. Gaithersburg, Md.: International Association of Chiefs of Police, 1970.

1651. Jensen, Clayne, and A. Garth Fisher. SCIENTIFIC BASIS OF ATHLETIC CONDITIONING. Philadelphia, Pa.: Lea and Febiger, 1972.

1652. Joint Commission on Corrections, Manpower and Training. OFFENDERS AS A CORRECTIONAL MANPOWER RESOURCE. Washington, D.C.: American Correctional Association, 1968.

1653. Kearney, Paul W. HOW TO DRIVE BETTER AND AVOID ACCIDENTS. New York, N.Y.: Thomas Y. Crowell Co., 1969.

1654. Kelley, Patrick. BUILDING SAFE DRIVING SKILLS. Palo Alto, Calif.: Fearon Publishers, 1972.

1655. Kim, Daeshik, and Tom Leland. KARATE AND PERSONAL DEFENSE. Dubuque, Iowa: William C. Brown, 1971.

★1656. Klotter, John C. TECHNIQUES FOR POLICE INSTRUCTORS. Springfield, Ill.: Charles C. Thomas, 1971.

1657. Koehler, W. R. THE KOEHLER METHOD OF GUARD DOG TRAINING. New York, N.Y.: Howell Book House, 1972.

1658. Koga, Robert K., and John Nelson. THE KOGA METHOD: POLICE WEAPONLESS CONTROL AND DEFENSE TECHNIQUES. Riverside, N.J.: Glencoe Press, 1967.

1659. Kudo, Kazuzo. DYNAMIC JUDO: GRAPPLING TECHNIQUES. San Francisco, Calif.: Japan Publications Trading Co., 1967.

1660. Leithe, Frederick E. JAPANESE HAND PISTOLS. Alhambra, Calif.: Borden Publishing, 1968.

1661. Levenson, William B., and Edward Stasheff. TEACHING THROUGH RADIO AND TELEVISION. Westport, Conn.: Greenwood Press, 1969.

1662. Masters, Robert. COMPLETE BOOK OF SELF-DEFENSE. Garden City, N.Y.: Doubleday and Co., 1968.

1663. Moore, Mary. MEDICAL EMERGENCY MANUAL: EMERGENCY MEDICINE. Baltimore, Md.: William and Wilkins, 1972.

1664. Nakayama, Masatoshi. DYNAMIC KARATE: INSTRUCTION BY THE MASTER. Palo Alto, Calif.: Kodansha International, U.S.A., 1967.

1665. Nonte, George. MODERN HANDLOADING. New York, N.Y.: Winchester Press, 1972.

1666. Nonte, George. SHOOTER'S BIBLE PISTOL AND REVOLVER GUIDE. Chicago, Ill.: Follett Publishing Co., 1969.

1667. Oyama, Masutatsu. ADVANCED KARATE. San Francisco, Calif.: Japan Publications Trading Co., 1970.

1668. Peel, John Donald. FUNDAMENTALS OF TRAINING FOR SECURITY OFFICERS: A COMPREHENSIVE GUIDE TO WHAT YOU SHOULD BE, KNOW AND DO TO HAVE A SUCCESSFUL CAREER AS A PRIVATE PATROLMAN OR SECURITY OFFICER. Springfield, Ill.: Charles C. Thomas, 1969.

1669. Pfluger, A. KARATE: BASIC PRINCIPLES. Scranton, Pa.: Barnes and Noble, 1970.

1670. POLICE EXPERIENCE FILM MODULES: (1) Fear and Anxiety, 10 min.; (2) Feeling Good, 9 min.; (3) Humiliation and Anger, 10 min. (16mm b&w). Gaithersburg, Md.: International Association of Chiefs of Police.

1671. POLICE SENSITIVITY TRAINING. (Cassette tape, 30 min.) North Hollywood, Calif.: Center for Cassette Studies.

1672. Popham, W. James. INSTRUCTIONAL OBJECTIVES. Chicago, Ill.: Rand McNally, 1969.

1673. RESCUE BREATHING. (Sound filmstrip, color.) Gaithersburg, Md.: International Association of Chiefs of Police.

1674. SAFE DRIVING TECHNIQUES. (Sound filmstrip, color). Gaithersburg, Md.: International Association of Chiefs of Police.

1675. Saunders, Blanche. THE COMPLETE BOOK OF DOG OBEDIENCE: A GUIDE FOR TRAINERS. New York, N.Y.: Howell Book House, 1972.

1676. SEVERE MENTAL ILLNESS. (Sound filmstrip, color.) Gaithersburg, Md.: International Association of Chiefs of Police.

1677. SHOCK. (Sound filmstrip, color.) Gaithersburg, Md.: International Association of Chiefs of Police.

1678. SHOOT/DON'T SHOOT. (16mm or videotape, color, 24 min.) Chicago, Ill.: Motorola Systems, Inc.

*1679. Siegel, Arthur I., and others. PROFESSIONAL POLICE-HUMAN RELATIONS TRAINING. Springfield, Ill.: Charles C. Thomas, 1970.

1680. Smith, Patrick D., and Robert C. Jones. POLICE ENGLISH: A MANUAL OF GRAMMAR, PUNCTUATION, AND SPELLING FOR POLICE OFFICERS. Springfield, Ill.: Charles C. Thomas, 1969.

1681. Spackman, Robert R., and William F. Vincent. PHYSICAL FITNESS IN LAW ENFORCEMENT: A GUIDE TO MORE EFFICIENT SERVICE. Carbondale, Ill.: South Illinois University Press, 1969.

1682. Stroh, Thomas F. THE USES OF VIDEO TAPE IN TRAINING AND DEVELOPMENT. Riverside, N.J.: American Management Association, 1968.

1683. Sylvain, George. DEFENSE AND CONTROL TACTICS. Englewood Cliffs, N.J.: Prentice Hall, 1971.

1684. TECHNIQUES OF ARREST I. (16mm or videotape, color, 20 min.) Chicago, Ill.: Motorola Systems, Inc.

1685. Tegner, Bruce. COMPLETE BOOK OF JUDO. Ventura, Calif.: Thor Publishing Co., 1967.

1686. Tegner, Bruce. DEFENSE TACTICS FOR LAW ENFORCEMENT. Ventura, Calif.: Thor Publishing Co., 1972.

1687. U. S. Army Department. SNIPER TRAINING AND EMPLOYMENT. Washington, D.C.: U. S. Government Printing Office, 1969.

1688. U. S. Law Enforcement Assistance Administration. IN-SERVICE TRAINING FOR PROBATION, PAROLE AND CORRECTIONAL PERSONNEL: A PLAN FOR ACTION. Washington, D.C.: U. S. Government Printing Office, 1968.

★1689. U. S. Law Enforcement Assistance Administration. POLICE TRAINING AND PERFORMANCE STUDY. Washington, D.C.: U. S. Government Printing Office, 1971.

1690. U. S. Law Enforcement Assistance Administration. TRAINING POLICE AS SPECIALISTS IN FAMILY CRISIS INTERVENTION. Washington, D.C.: U. S. Government Printing Office, 1970.

1691. U. S. National Highway Safety Bureau. BASIC TRAINING PROGRAM FOR EMERGENCY MEDICAL TECHNICIAN-AMBULANCE: CONCEPTS AND RECOMMENDATIONS. Washington, D.C.: U. S. Government Printing Office, 1970.

1692. U. S. National Highway Safety Bureau. BASIC TRAINING PROGRAM FOR EMERGENCY MEDICAL TECHNICIAN-AMBULANCE:

INSTRUCTOR'S LESSON PLANS. Washington, D.C.: U. S. Government Printing Office, 1970.

1693. U. S. National Highway Safety Bureau. ECONOMICS OF HIGHWAY EMERGENCY AMBULANCE SERVICES. Washington, D.C.: U. S. Government Printing Office, 1969.

1694. USE OF FIREARMS. (Sound filmstrip, color.) Gaithersburg, Md.: International Association of Chiefs of Police.

1695. Watson, Sam. DOGS FOR POLICE SERVICE: PROGRAMMING AND TRAINING. Springfield, III.: Charles C. Thomas, 1972.

1696. Wels, Byron G. FELL'S GUIDE TO GUNS AND HOW TO USE THEM SAFELY—LEGALLY—RESPONSIBLY. New York, N.Y.: Frederick Fell, 1969.

★1697. Weston, Paul B. COMBAT SHOOTING FOR POLICE. Springfield, III.: Charles C. Thomas, 1970.

1698. Wicks, Robert, and Ernest Josephs. TECHNIQUES IN INTERVIEWING FOR LAW ENFORCEMENT AND CORRECTIONS PERSONNEL: A PROGRAMMED TEXT. Springfield, III.: Charles C. Thomas, 1972.

1699. Young, Carl B. FIRST AID FOR EMERGENCY CREWS: A MANUAL ON EMERGENCY FIRST AID PROCEDURES FOR AMBULANCE CREWS, LAW ENFORCEMENT OFFICERS, FIRE SERVICE PERSONNEL, WRECKER DRIVERS, HOSPITAL STAFFS, INDUSTRY NURSES. Springfield, III.: Charles C. Thomas, 1970.

VICTIMLESS CRIME

See also Alcoholism   Judicial Process
         Behavioral and Social Science   Police Patrol Function
         Civil Rights   Support Services
         Classification of: Crime/Offenders   Training
         Drug: Information/Treatment

1700. Acton, William. PROSTITUTION. New York, N.Y.: Praeger Publishers, 1969.

1701. Douglas, Jack D. THE SOCIAL MEANINGS OF SUICIDE. Princeton, N.J.: Princeton University Press, 1970.

1702. Downing, A. B. EUTHANASIA AND THE RIGHT TO DEATH: THE CASE FOR VOLUNTARY EUTHANASIA. New York, N.Y.: Humanities Press, 1970.

1703. Greenwald, Harold. THE ELEGANT PROSTITUTE. New York, N.Y.: Ballantine Books, 1970.

1704. Grollman, Earl A. SUICIDE: PREVENTION, INTERVENTION, POSTVENTION. Boston, Mass.: Beacon Press, 1971.

★1705. Humphreys, Laud. TEAROOM TRADE: IMPERSONAL SEX IN PUBLIC PLACES. Chicago, Ill.: Aldine/Atherton, 1970.

1706. Keiser, R. Lincoln. THE VICE LORDS: WARRIORS OF THE STREETS. New York, N.Y.: Holt, Rinehart and Winston, 1969.

1707. Kuh, Richard H. FOOLISH FIGLEAVES. Riverside, N.J.: Macmillan Co., 1967.

1708. Leonard, Calista V. UNDERSTANDING AND PREVENTING SUICIDE. Springfield, Ill.: Charles C. Thomas, 1967.

1709. Masaryk, Thomas G. SUICIDE AND THE MEANING OF CIVILIZA- TION. Chicago, Ill.: University of Chicago Press, 1970.

1710. Nimmer, Raymond. TWO MILLION UNNECESSARY ARRESTS: REMOVING A SOCIAL SERVICE CONCERN FROM THE CRIM- INAL JUSTICE SYSTEM. Chicago, Ill.: American Bar Foundation, 1971.

1711. Norwick, Kenneth. PORNOGRAPHY: THE ISSUES AND THE LAW. New York, N.Y.: Public Affairs Commission, 1972.

1712. U.S. Obscenity and Pornography Commission. REPORT OF THE COMMISSION. Washington, D.C.: U.S. Government Printing Office, 1971.

1713. U.S. Obscenity and Pornography Commission. TECHNICAL REPORT OF THE COMMISSION ON OBSCENITY AND PORNOGRAPHY, VOL. III, THE MARKETPLACE: THE INDUSTRY. Washington, D.C.: U.S. Government Printing Office, 1971.

1714. U.S. Public Health Service. SUICIDE IN THE UNITED STATES— 1950-1964. Washington, D.C.: U.S. Government Printing Office, 1967.

★1715. William, John B., and E. R. Bloomquist. VICE AND ITS CONTROL. Riverside, N.J.: Glencoe Press, 1971.

1716. Winick, Charles, and Paul M. Kinsie. THE LIVELY COMMERCE: PROSTITUTION IN THE UNITED STATES. Cleveland, Ohio: Quadrangle Books, 1971.

1717. Wolff, Kurt. PATTERNS OF SELF DESTRUCTION: DEPRESSION AND SUICIDE. Springfield, Ill.: Charles C. Thomas, 1970.

1718. AMERICAN BAR ASSOCIATION JOURNAL. (1915) Ed. Richard B. Allen. American Bar Association, 1155 E. 60th St., Chicago, III. 60637 (available in microfilm).

1719. AMERICAN BEHAVIORAL SCIENTIST. (1957) Ed. Sara Miller McCune. Sage Publications, Inc., 275 S. Beverly Dr., Beverly Hills, Calif. 90212 (available in microform).

1720. AMERICAN CRIMINAL LAW QUARTERLY. (1962) Ed. Eugene T. Noonan. American Bar Association and University of Kansas School of Law, Section of Criminal Law, 1155 E. 60th St., Chicago, III. 60637.

1721. AMERICAN CRIMINOLOGIST. (1953) Ed. Wayne A. Forester. American Association of Criminology, Box 3014, University Station, Eugene, Ore. 97403.

1722. AMERICAN JOURNAL OF CORRECTION. (1920) Ed. Roberts J. Wright. American Correctional Association, 2642 University Ave., St. Paul, Minn. 55114.

1723. AMERICAN JOURNAL OF SOCIOLOGY. (1895) Ed. C. Arnold Anderson. University of Chicago Press, 5801 S. Ellis Ave., Chicago, III. 60637 (available on microfilm).

1724. AMERICAN SOCIOLOGICAL REVIEW. (1936) Ed. Karl F. Schuessler. American Sociological Association, 1001 Connecticut Ave., N.W., Washington, D.C. 20036.

1725. CENTER FOR LAW ENFORCEMENT RESEARCH INFORMATION. (1968) Ed. Quinn Tamm. International Association of Chiefs of Police, Gaithersburg, Md. 20760.

1726. CHICAGO POLICE STAR. Ed. Janet Dow. Chicago Police Department, Public Information Division, 1121 S. State St., Chicago, III. 60605.

1727. CRIME AND DELINQUENCY. (1955) Ed. Matt Matlin. National Council on Crime and Delinquency, 44 E. 23rd St., New York, N.Y. 10010.

1728. CRIME CONTROL DIGEST. (1967) Ed. James A. George. Sci/Tech Digests, Inc., 888 National Press Bldg., Washington, D.C. 20004.

1729. CRIMINAL LAW BULLETIN. (1970) Eds. Neil Fabricant and Joshua Koplovitz. Hanover Lamont Corporation, 89 Beach St., Boston, Mass. 02111.

1730. CRIMINOLOGY: AN INTERDISCIPLINARY JOURNAL. (1963) Ed. C. Ray Jeffery. Sage Publications, 275 S. Beverly Dr., Beverly Hills, Calif. 90212.

1731. DRUG DEPENDENCE. (1969) Eds. Sidney Cohen and David D. Swenson. National Clearinghouse for Mental Health Information, 5454 Wisconsin Ave., Chevy Chase, Md. 20015.

1732. DRUG INFORMATION BULLETIN. (1966) Ed. Don E. Francke. Drug Information Association, 112 Pavilion N., University Cincinnati, Medical Center, Cincinnati, Ohio 45229.

1733. ENFORCEMENT JOURNAL. (1962) Ed. Frank J. Schira. National Police Officers Association of America, 2801 E. Oakland Park Blvd., Ft. Lauderdale, Fla. 33306.

1734. F.B.I. LAW ENFORCEMENT BULLETIN. Federal Bureau of Investigation, U. S. Department of Justice, Washington, D.C. 20535.

1735. FEDERAL PROBATION: A JOURNAL OF CORRECTIONAL PHILOSOPHY AND PRACTICE. (1936) Ed. Victor H. Evjen. United States Courts, Administrative Office, Supreme Court Bldg., Washington, D.C. 20544.

1736. GRASSROOTS. (1970) Ed. Peter G. Hammond. National Coordinating Council on Drug Abuse Education and Information, Inc., 1211 Connecticut Ave., N.W., Washington, D.C. 20036.

1737. GUNS AND AMMO. (1958) Petersen Publishing Co., 8490 Sunset Blvd., Los Angeles, Calif. 90069.

1738. ISSUES IN CRIMINOLOGY. (1965) Ed. Frances S. Coles. University of California, 101 Haviland Hall, Berkeley, Calif. 94720 (available in microform).

1739. JOURNAL OF CRIMINAL LAW, CRIMINOLOGY AND POLICE SCIENCE. (1910) Ed. Fred E. Inbau. Williams and Wilkins Co., 428 E. Preston St., Baltimore, Md. 21202.

1740. JOURNAL OF PERSONALITY AND SOCIAL PSYCHOLOGY. (1965) Ed. Daniel Katz. American Psychological Association, 1200 17th St., N.W., Washington, D.C. 20036 (available in microform).

1741. JOURNAL OF RESEARCH IN CRIME AND DELINQUENCY. (1964) Ed. Dr. D. M. Grottfredson. National Council on Crime and Delinquency Research Center, Brinley Terrace, 609 2nd St., Davis, Calif. 95616 (available in microform).

1742. JOURNAL OF SOCIAL PSYCHOLOGY. (1929) Ed. Leonard W. Doob. Journal Press, 2 Commercial St., Provincetown, Mass. 02657.

1743. LAW AND ORDER. (1953) Ed. Frank G. MacAloon. Copp Organization, Inc., 37 W. 38th St., New York, N.Y. 10018.

1744. LAW OFFICER. (1968) Ed. Royce L. Givens. International Conference of Police Associations, 3000 France Ave. S., Minneapolis, Minn. 55416.

1745. LEGISLATIVE AND LITIGATION REPORT. International Association of Chiefs of Police, Gaithersburg, Md. 20760.

1746. LEGISLATIVE RESEARCH DIGEST. International Association of Chiefs of Police, Gaithersburg, Md. 20760.

1747. LAW ENFORCEMENT LEGAL REVIEW. (1972) International Association of Chiefs of Police, Gaithersburg, Md. 20760.

1748. MANAGEMENT REVIEW. (1923) Ed. E. M. Rosenthal. American Management Association, Inc., 135 W. 50th St., New York, N.Y. 10020 (available in microform).

1749. NARCOTICS CONTROL DIGEST. Ed. Richard J. O'Connell. Sci/Tech Digests, 888 National Press Bldg., Washington, D.C. 20004.

1750. PERSONNEL. (1919) Ed. Robert F. Guder. American Management Association, 135 W. 50th St., New York, N.Y. 10020 (available in microform).

1751. PERSONNEL ADMINISTRATOR. (1948) Ed. Samuel A. Jaeger. American Society for Personnel Administration, 52 E. Bridge St., Berea, Ohio 44017.

1752. PERSONNEL JOURNAL. (1922) Ed. A. C. Croft. Personnel Journal, Inc., Box 239, Swarthmore, Pa. 19081 (available in microform).

1753. POLICE. (1956) Ed. Charles C. Thomas, 735 N. Atlantic Blvd., Ft. Lauderdale, Fla. 33304.

1754. POLICE CHIEF. (1934) Ed. Quinn Tamm. International Association of Chiefs of Police, Gaithersburg, Md. 20760.

1755. POLICE TIMES. (1964) Ed. Gerald S. Arenberg. American Federation of Police, 1100 N.E. 125th St., North Miami, Fla. 33161.

1756. PROBATION AND PAROLE. (1969) Ed. Joseph Yomtov. New York State Probation and Parole Officers Association, Box 408, Madison Square Station, New York, N.Y. 10010.

1757. PUBLIC ADMINISTRATION REVIEW. (1940) Ed. Dwight Waldo. American Society for Public Administration, 1225 Connecticut Ave., N.W., Washington, D.C. 20036 (available in microform).

1758. PUBLIC MANAGEMENT. (1919) Eds. David S. Arnold and Marion C. Tureck. International City Management Association, 1140 Connecticut Ave., N.W., Washington, D.C. 20036 (available in microform).

1759. PUBLIC SAFETY LABOR REPORTER. International Association of Chiefs of Police, Gaithersburg, Md. 20760.

1760. SECURITY WORLD. (1964) Ed. Mary M. Hughes. Security World Publishing Co., 2639 S. La Cienega Blvd., Los Angeles, Calif. 90034 (available on microfilm).

1761. SOCIAL PROBLEMS. (1953). Ed. David Gold. Society for the Study of Social Problems, Executive Office, 1316-1/2 Mishawaka Ave., South Bend, Ind. 46615.

1762. SYSTEMS, TECHNOLOGY AND SCIENCE FOR LAW ENFORCE-MENT AND SECURITY, NEWSLETTER. (1969) Ed. Lowell H. Hattery. Lomond Systems, Inc., Mt. Airy, Md. 21771.

1763. TRAFFIC DIGEST AND REVIEW. (1953) Ed. Billie Watson. Traffic Institute, Northwestern University, 405 Church St., Evanston, Ill. 60204 (available in microform).

1764. TRAFFIC SAFETY. (1927) Ed. Angela Maher. National Safety Council, Inc., 425 N. Michigan Ave., Chicago, Ill. 60611.

SUBJECT/CONTENT INDICATORS—HIERARCHIC

Alcoholism

Alcohol and Drugs
Alcohol Chemical Testing
Alcohol Detoxification
Alcoholic
Alcoholism Causes

Diabetics
Drunk Offender Implied Consent
Drunk Offender Release
Revolving Door Process

Behavioral and Social Science

Adolescent Attitudes
Alienation
Antisocial Behavior
Attitude Towards Authority
Attitudes
Behavior Problems
Behavior Under Stress
Behavioral Research
Black Americans
Conflict Resolution
Discrimination
Group Behavior
Guided Group Interaction
Homosexuality
Indigents
Individual Behavior
Intelligence (IQ)
Interpersonal Relations
Juveniles
Learning and Conditioning
Mental Health and Disorders
Mental Retardation

Mexican Americans
Minorities
Motivation
Older Americans
Perception
Personality
Psychological Dependence
Psychology
Public Attitudes
Puerto Rican Americans
Race Relations
Self Mutilation
Sexual Behavior
Social Change
Social Work
Social Worker
Socioculture
Sociology
Treatment and Rehabilitation
Venereal Disease
White Americans

Civil Rights

Bill of Rights
Capital Punishment
Civil Liberties
Constitutional Rights
Cruel and Unusual Punishment
Ex-Offender Rights
Fair Trial—Free Press
Freedom of Expression and
    Association

Invasion of Privacy
Offender Rights
Prisoner Rights
Right to Counsel
Rights of Minors
Rights of the Accused
Speedy Trial

Classification of Crime

Abortion
Aggravated Assault
Arson
Assassination
Assault
Auto Related Crimes
Auto Theft
Bank Check Abuses
Bomb Incidents and Threats
Bribery
Burglary
Conspiracy
Contempt of Congress
Contempt of Court
Counterfeiting
Credit Card Offenses
Crimes Against Children
Craimes Against Persons
Crimes Against Property
Customs Violations
Dealing in Stolen Goods
Driving Under the Influence
Driving Without Owners Consent
Embezzlement
Escape
Espionage
Euthanasia
Extortion
False Personation
False Pretenses
Federal Law Violations
Felony
Forgery
Fraud
Hijacking

Homicide
Immigration Offenses
Index Crimes
Jury Tampering
Juvenile Status Offenses
Kidnapping
Larceny
Libel
Liquor Law Violations
Manslaughter
Misdemeanor
Narcotics Violations
Obstructing Justice
Passport Offenses
Perjury
Piracy
Rape
Resisting Arrest
Robbery
Sabotage
Sex Crimes
Shoplifting
Smuggling
Sodomy
Statutory Rape
Stranger to Stranger Crime
Suicide
Swindling
Tax Evasion
Theft
Treason
Vandalism
Violent Crimes
Weapons Offenses
White Collar Crime

Classification of Offenders

Adult Offender
Amateur Offender
Female Offender
First Offender
Habitual Offender
Male Offender

Mentally Ill Offender
Professional Criminal
Recidivist
Violent Offender
Young Adult Offenders
Youthful Offender

Communications (Data)

Air-To-Ground Communications
Analog Voice Transmission
ASCII
Baudot Code
CCTV (Closed Circuit Television)
Civil Defense Communications
Communication Interference
Communication Systems
Communications Center
Data Transmission
Decoding
Digital Communications
Digital Inquiry—Voice Answerback
Digital Overlays
Dispatching System
Duplex Operation
Emergency Communications
Emergency Operations Center (EOC)
Encoding
Multi-Channel System
Personal Radio Communications
Point-To-Point Communications
Police Communications Network
Radio Ten Signals
Simplex Operation
Telecommunications
Telephone Communications
Television Communications
Transmission Security
UHF (Ultrahigh Frequency)
VHF (Very High Frequency)
Voice Transmission
Wave Propagation Analysis

Communications (Visual)

Related content indicators are found under Communications (Data) and Communications Equipment.

Communications (Voice)

Related content indicators are found under Communications (Data) and Communications Equipment.

Communications (Equipment)

Antenna
Citizen Radio Band
Communication Channel
Communication Channel Allocation
Communication Vans
Data Collection Devices
Digital Message Entry Device
Facsimile Equipment
FCC Regulations
Frequency Allocations
Mobile Radio Equipment
Mobile Relay Stations
Mobile Teleprinter
MODEM (Modulator-Demodulator)
Network Configuration
Police Radio Frequencies
Radio Base Station
Radio Call Box
Radio Channel Congestion
Radio Repeaters
Random Access Equipment
Remote Terminals
Telephone Data Set
Teletypewriter
Transmitter-Receiver

Community Based Corrections (Adult)

Graduated Release
Halfway Houses
Juvenile Foster Homes
Juvenile Group Houses

Study Release
Work Release
Youth Services Bureau

Community Based Corrections (Juvenile)

Applicable content indicators are found under Community Relations.

Community Involvement

Related content indicators are located under Community Relations.

Community Relations

Citizen Advisory Committees
Citizen Associations
Citizen Grievances
Citizen Legal Problems
Citizen Police Observer Program
Community Action Program
Community Conflict
Community Resources
Community Support
Crisis Intervention

Media Support
Police Business Cooperation
Police Community Relations
Police Juvenile Relations
Police School Relations
Volunteer Programs
Volunteers
Youth Groups
Youth Volunteers

Correctional Institutions (Adult)

Confinement Facility
Conjugal Visits
Correctional Facility
Correctional Reform
Federal Penitentiary
Furloughs
Inmate Compensation
Inmate Organizations
Inmate Programs
Inmate Staff Ratio
Inmate Staff Relations
Inmate Work

Inmates
Juvenile Correctional Facility
Juvenile Detention Facility
Maximum Security
Medium Security
Minimum Security
Overcrowding
Prerelease Program
Prison Farms
Violent Inmate
Work Camps

Correctional Institutions (Juvenile)

Related content indicators are listed under Correctional Institutions (Adult).

Court Management and Operation

Assignment of Court Cases
Case Scheduling
Continuances
Court Administrators
Court Calendar Control
Court Delay

Court Dockets
Court Executive
Court Records
Court Reporting
Court Security
Courts

Court Structure

Appellate Court
Court Reorganization
Courts of General Jurisdiction
Courts of Limited Jurisdiction
Family Court
Federal Court

Municipal Court
State Courts
Traffic Court
Trial Court
US Supreme Court

Crime Deterrence and Prevention

Bomb Detection
Citizens Crime Precautions
Countermeasures Operations
Crime Control Programs

Gun Control
Punishment
Security Codes and Ordinances

Criminal Investigation

Apprehension
Arrest
Crime Scene Search
Criminal Records
Electronic Surveillance
Evidence Preservation
Informers
Intelligence Acquisition
International Police Activities
Interview and Interrogation

Manhunt
Missing Person Investigation
Offender
Organized Crime Investigation
Postarrest Procedures
Search and Seizure
Search Warrant
Surveillance
Suspect Identification
Undercover Activity

Criminalistics

Automated Fingerprint Processing
Autopsy
Ballistics
Blood Analysis
Bullet Hole Identification
Coroners
Covert Markings
Crime Laboratories
Crime Laboratory Equipment
Dental Analysis
Document Analysis
Evidence Collection
Evidence Identification
Fingerprints
Firearms Identification
Fluorescence Evaluation
Forensic Medicine
Gas Chromatography
Glass Analysis

Hair and Fiber Analysis
Handwriting Analysis
Metal Identification
Mineral Analysis
Mobile Laboratory
Neutron Activation Analysis
Paint Analysis
Photography
Poisons
Polygraphy
Pyrolysis
Shoe Prints and Tire Treads
Spectrometry
Toolmark Identification
Trace Evidence Comparison
Ultraviolet Techniques
Victim Identification
Voice Identification
Wood Examination

Criminology

Applicable content indicators are found under Crime Causes, Behavioral and Social Science, and Crime Deterrence.

Domestic Relations

Child Abuse
Family Crisis

Juvenile Dependency and Neglect
Marital Problems

Drug Information

Addict Characteristics
Addiction
Amphetamines
Barbituates
Cocaine
Drug Abuse
Drug Abuse Causes
Drug Abuse Effects
Drug Dealing
Drug Detection
Drug Newsletter

Drug Prevention Programs
Drug Regulation
Drug Research
Drug Sources
Drug Use
Drugmobile
Hallucinogens
Hashish
Heroin
Intoxicant Inhalation
LSD

Drug Information (Cont'd)

Marijuana
Methadone
Opiates

Peyote
Tranquilizers

Drug Treatment

Cyclazozine
Drug Detoxification
Drug Involuntary Treatment
Drug Treatment Programs

Drug Urinalysis
Drug Voluntary Treatment
Drug Withdrawal
Methadone Maintenance

Education

Accreditation
Adult Education
Certificate Programs
Correspondence Course
Criminal Justice Education
Curriculum
Degree Programs
Experimental Education
Fellowships and Scholarships
Intern Programs
Jurisprudence
Law Degree

Law Enforcement Education
Law Student Aides
Law Student Defender Programs
Law Student Prosecutor Programs
LEEP (Law Enforcement Education
    Program)
Mobile Classrooms
Non-Degree Course
Police Science Education
Refresher Courses
SATE (Self Advancement Through
    Education)

Explosives and Weapons

Use this subject indicator for devices and materials utilized in an illicit manner.

Blasting Accessories
Bombs
Burglary Tools

Illicit Chemicals
Illicit Firearms
Incendiary Devices

Information Systems

Adult Felony System
ALERT (Auto Law Enforcement
    RPTG Tech)
ALPS (Automatic License Plate
    Scanning)

Auto Theft Inquiry Systems
Automated Court Systems
Automated Jury Selection Systems
Automated Modus Operandi Systems
Automated Police Information

Information Systems (Cont'd)

AWDI (Automated Worthless Document Index)
Cincinnati Information System (CINSY)
Computer Aided Car Control Systems
Computer Aided Operations
Computer Mapping Systems
Correctional Information System
Court Calendar Models
Court Case Flow Models
Court Data Flow Simulation
Court Simulation (Courtsim)
Crime Control Model
Criminal Justice Information Systems
Data Integrity
Data Security
Due Process Model
ERIC
General Purpose System Simulator (GPSS)

Legal Reference Services
LETS (Law Enforcement Teleprinter System)
Management Information Systems
Modus Operandi Data Systems (MODS)
Name Identification
NCIC (National Criminal Information Center)
Police Information Systems
Prosecution Model
SEARCH (Sys Electr Anal & Retr Crim Hist)
SIMBAD (Simul Basis for Social Agents Dec)
Simulation Models
Synagraphic Computer Mapping (SYMAP)
Theft Inquiry Systems
Video Tape Applications
WALES (Wash Area Law Enforcement System)

Information: Systems/Software

These content indicators are located under Information Systems.

Jails

Jail Administration
Jail Admissions

Jail Reform

Judicial Process

Adjudication
Arraignment
Civil Commitment
Confession
Courtroom Decorum
Criminal Responsibility
Cross-Examination
Detainers
Detention

Double Jeopardy
Due Process
Evidence Presentation
Fines
Injunction
Joinder and Severance
Judge
Judge Censure and Removal
Judge Communications with Jurors

Judicial Process (Cont'd)

Judge Selection
Judge Sentencing Discretion
Judicial Conduct and Ethics
Judicial Decisions
Judicial Review
Jurisdiction
Jury
Justice of Peace
Juvenile Court Diversion
Juvenile Court Intake
Juvenile Court Procedures
Military Justice
Multiple Convictions
Post Conviction Procedures
Preliminary Hearing

Pretrial Discovery
Pretrial Procedures
Rules of Evidence
Self Incrimination
Sentencing
Sentencing Alternatives
Subpoenas
Summons
Testimony
Trial Preparation
Trials
Warrant
Witness
Witness Protection

Juvenile Court

Applicable content indicators are found under Court and Judicial sections.

Juvenile Delinquency

Dropouts
Emotionally Disburbed Delinquent
Juvenile Delinquency Factors
Juvenile Delinquency Prediction
Juvenile Delinquency Prevention

Juvenile Delinquents
Juvenile Detention
Juvenile Experimental Groups
Juvenile Processing
Juvenile Status Offenders

Laws and Statutes

Citizenship Laws
Civil Rights Laws
Common Law
Copyright Laws
Criminal Code
Drug Laws
Executive Orders
Federal Bail Reform Act
Federal Code
Federal Drug Laws
Firearms Acts
Internal Revenue Laws

International Agreements
Juvenile Code
Law Enforcement Assistance Act
Licensing and Regulation
Liquor Control Laws
Omnibus Crime Control and Safe
    Streets Act
Search and Seizure Laws
Sovereign Immunity
State Laws
Voting Legislation

Organized Crime

Black Market
Corruption of Public Officials
Criminal Infiltration of Business
Enforcer
Labor Racketeering
Loan Sharking
Loan Sharks
Organized Crime Boss
Organized Crime Code of Conduct
Organized Crime Confederation
Organized Crime Conferences
Organized Crime Corrupter
Organized Crime Counselor

Organized Crime Families
Organized Crime Financial Adviser
Organized Crime Financial Power
Organized Crime Growth
Organized Crime Hierarchy
Organized Crime Impact
Organized Crime Intelligence
Organized Crime Membership
Organized Crime Power Groups
Organized Crime Profit
Organized Crime Underboss
Unlawful Compensation

Personnel Administration

Career Development
Caseload
Discipline
Educational Levels
Fringe Benefits
Injured on Duty
Interagency Transfers
Job Analysis
Labor Relations
Leadership
Minority Employment
Morale
Occupational Mobility
Ombudsman
Paraprofessional
Part-Time Personnel
Pay Rates
Performance Requirements
Personnel

Personnel Minimum Standards
Personnel Probation
Personnel Retention
Personnel Selection
Personnel Shortages
Professional Organizations
Professionalization
Promotion Policy
Psychological Testing and Measure-
    ment
Recruitment
Retirement and Pension
Staff Client Relationship
Supervision
Turnover Rates
Unions
Work Load
Work Schedules
Youth Employment

Planning and Evaluation

This section includes indicators related to General Management, Financial
Management, and Research and Development.

Architectural Design
Capital Investment
Correctional Planning

Cost Benefit Analysis
Criminal Justice System
Critical Path Method

Planning and Evaluation (Cont'd)

Environmental Quality
Estimating Methods
Evaluation
Facilities
Facility Conditions
Federal Aid
Impact Cities
Law Enforcement
Line-Item Budget
Long Range Prediction
Management Theories
Mathematical Model
Modeling Techniques
Operating Costs
Operations Management

Pert
Pilot Cities
Planning
Policy
PPBS (Planning-Programming-
    Budgeting Systems)
Prediction Model
Program Coordination
Program Financing
Records Management
Regionalization
Research Methods
Research Organizations
Systems Analysis
Urban Planning

Police Equipment

Aerosol Projectors
Ammunition
Armored Vehicles
Automobile Surveillance Device
Automobiles
Bicycles
Body Armor
Bomb Disposal Equipment
Electronic Surveillance Devices
Equipment Maintenance and
    Storage
Headgear
Helicopters
Motorcycles

Motorscooters
Night Vision Devices
Nonlethal Weapons
Police Vans
Police Weapons
Resuscitators
Riot Shields
Searchlights
STOL (Short Takeoff and
    Landing)
Traffic Control Equipment
Uniforms
Vehicle Equipment

Police Internal Affairs

Abuse of Authority
Background Investigations
Civilian Review Boards
Code of Ethics
Complaints Against Police
Off-Duty Offenses
On-Duty Offenses
Police Appeal Rights

Police Brutality
Police Commendation
Police Corruption
Police Internal Investigations
Police Internal Security and
    Inspection
Police Reprimand
Police Trial Board

Police Management

Auxiliary Police
Deployment
Disaster Procedures
Police Cadets
Police Chief
Police Consolidation
Police Court Relations
Police Discretion
Police Effectiveness

Police Legal Advisers
Police Legal Limitations
Police Press Relations
Police Recruit
Police Response Time
Police Responsibilities
Police Services Coordination
Policewoman
Public Safety Coordination

Police Organization

Bomb Disposal Unit
Citizen Service Unit
Civil Disturbance Unit
County Police
FCIU (Family Crisis Intervention Unit)
Federal Law Enforcement Agencies
Intelligence Unit
Metropolitan Police
Municipal Police
Plain Clothes Operations

Police Central Control
Police Youth Unit
Private Police
Records Section
Sheriff
Special Purpose Public Police
State Police
Tactical Unit
Township Police
Vice Unit
Village Police

Police Patrol Function

Aerial Patrol
Bicycle Patrol
Bomb Disposal Procedures
Citation
Citizens Arrest
Crime Detection
Emergency Rescues
Field Interrogation and Interview
Foot Patrol

Hot Pursuit
Motor Patrol
Patrol Procedures
Patrol Unit Status
Police Dog Utilization
Police Reports
Police Safety
Team Policing

Police Traffic Function

Accident Investigation
Driver Road Check
Emergency Vehicles
Highway Patrol
Highway Safety

Hit and Run Investigation
License Check
Traffic Direction and Control
Traffic Surveillance
Vehicle Safety Inspection

Probation and Parole (Adult)

Informal Probation
Parole
Parole Agencies
Parole Board
Parole Conditions
Parole Hearing
Parolees
Probation
Probation and Parole Decision
    Making
Probation and Parole Investiga-
    tions
Probation and Parole Records
Probation and Parole Services
Probation and Parole Subsidy
Probation Conditions
Probation Hearing
Probationer
Recidivism

Probation and Parole (Juvenile)

Related content indicators are found under Probation and Parole (Adult).

Prosecution

Attorneys General
Defective Indictments
Grand Jury
Indictment or Information
Investigative Powers
Plea or Disposition Negotiations
Prosecuting Attorney
Prosecution Appeals
Prosecutory Discretion

Public Information and Education

Applicable content indicators are listed under Reference Materials.

Reference Material

Agency Directories
Audiovisual Material
Bibliography
Case Study
Congressional Information
Critique
Fiction
Film
Grants and Contracts
History
Legislation
Library
Model Law
Organization Study
Periodical
Procedure Manual
Proceedings
Public Information
Public Relations Programs
Publications List
Questionnaire
Reading List
Standards and Goals
State Plan
State-of-the-Art Review
Summary

Reference Material (Cont'd)

Television

Terminology Definitions

Theory

Training Manual

Research and Development

Related content indicators are located under Planning and Evaluation.

Riot Control and Urban Disorders

Armed Forces

Civil Disobedience

Civil Disturbance

Collective Violence

Confrontation Tactics

Crowd Behavior

Crowd Control

Curfew

Decontamination

Defiance of Law

Emergency Detention

First Aid

Mass Arrest Procedures

Media Coverage

Mob Action Coercion

Mob Infiltration

Participant Identification

Riot Causation

Riot Control Agents

Riot Control Principles

Riot Patterns

Riot Prevention

Rumor Control

Sniper Apprehension

Toxic Reactions

Urban Guerrilla Warfare

Urban Riots

Security Systems

Aircraft Security

Airport Security

Alarm Systems

Facility Security

Industrial Security

Lighting

Locks

Security Surveillance Systems

Statistics

Arrest Statistics

Clearance Rates

Corrections Statistics

Court Statistics

Crime Statistics

Crime Surveys

Criminal Statistics

Estimated Crime Incident

Fatalities

Frequency Distribution

International Crime Rates

National Crime Statistics

Offense Statistics

Parole Statistics

Population Profiles

Prisoner Statistics

Probation Statistics

Rural Statistics and Studies

Statistics (Cont'd)

Standard Metropolitan Statisti-
  cal Area
Statistical Analysis
Statistical Methods

Survey
UCR (Uniform Crime Reports)
Urban Statistics and Studies
Violent Crime Statistics

Student Disorders

Campus Authority
Campus Revolutionaries
Demonstrator Arrests
Negotiation
Outside Agitators

Student Discourse
Student Dissent
Student Expulsion
Student Forcible Control
Student Grievances

Support Services

Child Care
Civil Defense
Community Treatment Center
Consumer Protection
Counseling
Counselors
Emergency Telephone Number
Employment Service
Ex-Offender Employment
Exercise Facilities
Family Counseling
Fire Department
Followup Contacts
Food Service
Group Therapy

Hotline
Indigenous Citizen Aides
Legal Services
Medical and Dental Services
Milieu Therapy
Psychiatric Services
Psychiatry
Recreation
Referral Services
Religious Programs
Residential Center
Transportation Services
Treatment Offender Matching
Welfare Services

Training

Correctional Staff Training
Course Material
Custodial Officer Training
Driver Training
Effective Communications Training
First Aid Training
Foreign Language Training
Inservice Training
Instructor Selection
Judicial Training Courses

Juvenile Procedures Training
Legal Training
Lesson Plans
Management and Administrative
  Training
Minimum Basic Training
PACT (Pa Adult Correctional
  Training)
Physical Training
Police Academy

Training (Cont'd)

Police Training
Regional Training Centers
Remedial Education
Self Defense Training
Self Instruction Materials
Staff Development Training

Supervisory Training
Training Equipment
Vocational Training
Volunteer Training
Workshops and Seminars

Victimless Crime

Adultery
Bootlegging
Disorderly Conduct
Drunkenness
Indecency
Pandering

Pornography
Prostitution
Street Solicitation
Vagrancy
Vice

AUTHOR INDEX

Aaronson, Bernard, 745
Abbott, David W., 30
Abernathy, M. Glenn, 369
Abraham, Henry J., 876
Abrahams, Samuel, 732
Abrahamsen, David, 31
Abrams, Charles, 1431
Abt, Lawrence, 743
Acton, William, 1700
Adams, Brian C., 1600
Adams, Thomas, 1177-78
Adams, Thomas E., 1326
Adams, Thomas F., 467
Adrian, Charles, 32
Advena, Jean, 1432
Advisory Committee on Inter-
  governmental Relations, 33
Ahern, James, 1179
Ahlstrom, Winton, 989
Aiken, Michael, 34
Al-Anon Family Group, 1
Alex, Nicholas, 1102
Alexander, Alfred, 401
Alexander, Clifton, 746
Alexander, Sandy, 746
Alexander, Theron, 35
Alinsky, Saul, 36
Allen, Clifford, 37
Allen, Gary, 38
Allen, Merrill J., 1378
Allen, Richard, 877
Allington, Thomas, 523
Allsop, Kenneth, 39
Altbach, P. G., 1589
American Bar Association, 878-81,
  1055, 1103, 1241, 1407, 1421,
  1570
American Correctional Associa-
  tion, 1433
American Enterprise Institute for
  Public Policy Research, 1180
American Friends Service
  Committee, 540
American Humane Society, 402
American Medical Association, 2
American National Red Cross, 1619
American Society for Training and
  Development, 1620
Amir, Menachem, 403
Amos, William E., 990

Anastasi, Anne, 1104
Anderson, S., 40
Anthony, Earl, 41
Applegate, Rex, 1242
Arco Editorial Board, 1105-1108
Argyris, Chris, 42, 1109
Arm, Walter, 1110
Armour, David, 851
Arnold, David, 43
Arnold, William R., 1408
Aroeste, Jean, 1453
Aronfreed, Justin, 44
Arons, H., 573
Arther, Richard O., 574
Arthur D. Little, Inc., 1379
Artst, Eric, 185
Asch, Sidney, 370
Ashley-Montagu, M. F., 45
Ashman, Allan, 1056
Aspen, Marvin, 1067
Association of the Bar of the City of New
  York. Special Committee on Radio,
  Television and the Administration of
  Justice, 371
Aubrey, Arthur, 577
Aukofer, Frank, 46
Aussieker, M. W., 1111
Avedon, Donald, 852

Bacon, Margaret, 991
Baer, Walter E., 1112
Baird, Russell N., 497
Baker, Sara, 547
Ball, John, 747
Banfield, Edward C., 47
Banki, I. S., 1434
Banovetz, James, 48
Banton, Michael, 49
Barbara, Dominick A., 50
Barber, Bernard, 748
Barber, Theodore Xenophen, 749
Barbour, Floyd, 51
Bardis, Panos, 1571
Barnard, Chester, 1280
Barnes, Frank C., 1243
Barnes, Robert, 404
Barron, Milton L., 52
Bartlett, Eric, 1621
Barton, Allen H., 53

TITLE INDEX